To Ryan—
Hope you enjoy
this!
Love,
Mommy
8-27-07

ods · Michael Jackson · Ethelred the Unready · Elvis Presley · Ern
ingway · Bill Gates · Buffalo Bill Cody · Mia Hamm · Bill Clinton · Joan
· Billie Holiday · Al Capone · Leif Ericsso · Jane Austen · Muhammad
andas Gandhi · Orson Welles · Lola Montez · John Wilkes Booth · Y
garin · Jackie Robinson · Anne Boleyn · Harriet Tubman · Ludwig
ethoven · Babe Ruth · Thomas Jefferson · Martin Luther King Jr. ·
hrig · Jeannette Rankin · Michelangelo · Neil Armstrong · Amelia Earh
erdinand Magellan · Harriet Beecher Stowe · Christopher Reeve · Jar
ok · Sir Isaac Newton · Henry Ford · Anne Hutchinson · Vladimir Ily
in · Theodore Roosevelt · Karl Marx · Julius Caesar · Leonardo da V
immy Carter · Dwight D. Eisenhower · Queen Liliuokalani · Rachel Cars
George Washington · Geronimo · Charlemagne · Clara Barton · Rich
on · Benito Mussolini · Alfred Nobel · Nikita Khrushchev · Dou
cArthur · Zachary Taylor · Tamerlane · Edgar Rice Burroughs · Will
ary Harrison · Galileo Galilei · Golda Meir · Douglas MacArthur · N
e-tung · Ronald Reagan · Katharine Hepburn · Henry Fonda · Sir Wins
rchill · John Glenn · William Randolph Hearst · Grandma Moses · Aa
r · George Burns · Marshal Tito · Thomas Edison · Marshal Pétai
trand Russell · Oliver Wendell Holmes Jr. · Bob Hope · Connie Mac
nk Lloyd Wright · Pablo Picasso · Louis XIV · Wolfgang Amadeus Mozar
rley Temple · William Bligh · Tiger Woods · Michael Jackson · Ethel
e Unready · Elvis Presley · Ernest Hemingway · Bill Gates · Buffalo
dy · Mia Hamm · Bill Clinton · Joan of Arc · Billie Holiday · Al Capone · L
csso · Jane Austen · Muhammad Ali · Mohandas Gandhi · Orson Welles · L
ntez · John Wilkes Booth · Yury Gagarin · Jackie Robinson · Anne Bol
arriet Tubman · Ludwig van Beethoven · Babe Ruth · Thomas Jeffersc
rtin Luther King Jr. · Lou Gehrig · Jeannette Rankin · Michelangelo ·
nstrong · Amelia Earhart · Ferdinand Magellan · Harriet Beecher St
nristopher Reeve · James Cook · Sir Isaac Newton · Henry Ford · A
chinson · Vladimir Ilyich Lenin · Theodore Roosevelt · Karl Marx · J
esar · Leonardo da Vinci · Jimmy Carter · Dwight D. Eisenhowe
een Liliuokalani · Rachel Carson · George Washington · Geronim
arlemagne · Clara Barton · Richard Nixon · Benito Mussolini · Alf

when i was *your* age

Irreverent

An ^ Guide to Who Did What
and When, at Every Age
(Well, Only 4-90)

Mark Washburn

SOURCEBOOKS, INC.®
NAPERVILLE, ILLINOIS

Published by Sourcebooks, Inc.
P.O. Box 4410, Naperville, Illinois 60567-4410
(630) 961-3900
Fax: (630) 961-2168
www.sourcebooks.com

Library of Congress Cataloging-in-Publication Data

Washburn, Mark.
When I was your age—: a guide to who did what, and when / by Mark Washburn.
p. cm.
ISBN-13: 978-1-4022-0713-6
ISBN-10: 1-4022-0713-1
1. Biography. 2. Celebrities—Biography. I. Title.

CT104.W325 2006
920.02—dc22

2005033007

Printed and bound in China
LEO 10 9 8 7 6 5 4 3 2 1

dedication

For Charles Grassle, Paul Kocher,
Gail Beitelman, Al Mann, and Joe Sapone,
who taught me history long ago,
when there was less of it.

ds · Michael Jackson · Ethelred the Unready · Elvis Presley · Ern
ingway · Bill Gates · Buffalo Bill Cody · Mia Hamm · Bill Clinton · Joan
· Billie Holiday · Al Capone · Leif Ericsso · Jane Austen · Muhammad
andas Gandhi · Orson Welles · Lola Montez · John Wilkes Booth · y
garin · Jackie Robinson · Anne Boleyn · Harriet Tubman · Ludwig
thoven · Babe Ruth · Thomas Jefferson · Martin Luther King Jr. · L
rig · Jeannette Rankin · Michelangelo · Neil Armstrong · Amelia Earh
erdinand Magellan · Harriet Beecher Stowe · Christopher Reeve · Jar
k · Sir Isaac Newton · Henry Ford · Anne Hutchinson · Vladimir Ily
in · Theodore Roosevelt · Karl Marx · Julius Caesar · Leonardo da Vi
mmy Carter · Dwight D. Eisenhower · Queen Liliuokalani · Rachel Cars
eorge Washington · Geronimo · Charlemagne · Clara Barton · Rich
on · Benito Mussolini · Alfred Nobel · Nikita Khrushchev · Doug
Arthur · Zachary Taylor · Tamerlane · Edgar Rice Burroughs · Will
ry Harrison · Galileo Galilei · Golda Meir · Douglas MacArthur · M
-tung · Ronald Reagan · Katharine Hepburn · Henry Fonda · Sir Wins
rchill · John Glenn · William Randolph Hearst · Grandma Moses · Aar
r · George Burns · Marshal Tito · Thomas Edison · Marshal Pétai
trand Russell · Oliver Wendell Holmes Jr. · Bob Hope · Connie Mac
nk Lloyd Wright · Pablo Picasso · Louis XIV · Wolfgang Amadeus Mozar
-ley Temple · William Bligh · Tiger Woods · Michael Jackson · Ethel
Unready · Elvis Presley · Ernest Hemingway · Bill Gates · Buffalo
y · Mia Hamm · Bill Clinton · Joan of Arc · Billie Holiday · Al Capone · L
sso · Jane Austen · Muhammad Ali · Mohandas Gandhi · Orson Welles · L
tez · John Wilkes Booth · Yury Gagarin · Jackie Robinson · Anne Bole
rriet Tubman · Ludwig van Beethoven · Babe Ruth · Thomas Jefferso
tin Luther King Jr. · Lou Gehrig · Jeannette Rankin · Michelangelo · M
strong · Amelia Earhart · Ferdinand Magellan · Harriet Beecher Sto
ristopher Reeve · James Cook · Sir Isaac Newton · Henry Ford · An
chinson · Vladimir Ilyich Lenin · Theodore Roosevelt · Karl Marx · Ju
sar · Leonardo da Vinci · Jimmy Carter · Dwight D. Eisenhower
en Liliuokalani · Rachel Carson · George Washington · Geronimo
rlemagne · Clara Barton · Richard Nixon · Benito Mussolini · Alfr

contents

Sacagawea	age 17
Billie Holiday	age 18
Al Capone	age 19
Leif Ericsson	age 20
Jane Austen	age 21
Muhammad Ali	age 22
Mohandas Gandhi	age 23
Charlie Chaplin	age 24
Lola Montez	age 25
John Wilkes Booth	age 26
Marilyn Monroe	age 27
Jackie Robinson	age 28
Anne Boleyn	age 29
Harriet Tubman	age 30
Ludwig van Beethoven	age 31
Babe Ruth	age 32
Thomas Jefferson	age 33
Martin Luther King Jr.	age 34
Lou Gehrig	age 35
Jeannette Rankin	age 36
Michelangelo	age 37
Neil Armstrong	age 38

Amelia Earhart	age 39
Ferdinand Magellan	age 40
Harriet Beecher Stowe	age 41
Rosa Parks	age 42
James Cook	age 43
Sir Isaac Newton	age 44
Henry Ford	age 45
Sir Winston Churchill	age 46
Vladimir Ilyich Lenin	age 47
Theodore Roosevelt	age 48
William Shakespeare	age 49
Julius Caesar	age 50
Leonardo da Vinci	age 51
Jimmy Carter	age 52
Dwight D. Eisenhower	age 53
Queen Liliuokalani	age 54
Rachel Carson	age 55
George Washington	age 56
Geronimo	age 57
Charlemagne	age 58
Clara Barton	age 59
Richard Nixon	age 60

Benito Mussolini	age 61
Alfred Nobel	age 62
Nikita Khrushchev	age 63
Douglas MacArthur	age 64
Zachary Taylor	age 65
Tamerlane	age 66
Edgar Rice Burroughs	age 67
William Henry Harrison	age 68
Galileo Galilei	age 69
Golda Meir	age 70
Douglas MacArthur	age 71
Mao Zedong	age 72
Ronald Reagan	age 73
Katharine Hepburn	age 74
Henry Fonda	age 75
Sir Winston Churchill	age 76
John Glenn	age 77
William Randolph Hearst	age 78
Grandma Moses	age 79
Aaron Burr	age 80
George Burns	age 81
Marshal Tito	age 82

ods · Michael Jackson · Ethelred the Unready · Elvis Presley · Er
mingway · Bill Gates · Buffalo Bill Cody · Mia Hamm · Bill Clinton · Joar
c · Billie Holiday · Al Capone · Leif Ericsso · Jane Austen · Muhammad
handas Gandhi · Orson Welles · Lola Montez · John Wilkes Booth ·
agarin · Jackie Robinson · Anne Boleyn · Harriet Tubman · Ludwig
ethoven · Babe Ruth · Thomas Jefferson · Martin Luther King Jr. ·
ehrig · Jeannette Rankin · Michelangelo · Neil Armstrong · Amelia Earl
Ferdinand Magellan · Harriet Beecher Stowe · Christopher Reeve · Ja
ok · Sir Isaac Newton · Henry Ford · Anne Hutchinson · Vladimir Il
nin · Theodore Roosevelt · Karl Marx · Julius Caesar · Leonardo da V
Jimmy Carter · Dwight D. Eisenhower · Queen Liliuokalani · Rachel Car
Seorge Washington · Geronimo · Charlemagne · Clara Barton · Ric
xon · Benito Mussolini · Alfred Nobel · Nikita Khrushchev · Dou
cArthur · Zachary Taylor · Tamerlane · Edgar Rice Burroughs · W
nry Harrison · Galileo Galilei · Golda Meir · Douglas MacArthur ·
e-tung · Ronald Reagan · Katharine Hepburn · Henry Fonda · Sir Win
urchill · John Glenn · William Randolph Hearst · Grandma Moses · Ac
rr · George Burns · Marshal Tito · Thomas Edison · Marshal Pét
rtrand Russell · Oliver Wendell Holmes Jr. · Bob Hope · Connie Ma
ank Lloyd Wright · Pablo Picasso · Louis XIV · Wolfgang Amadeus Moza
irley Temple · William Bligh · Tiger Woods · Michael Jackson · Ethe
e Unready · Elvis Presley · Ernest Hemingway · Bill Gates · Buffalo
dy · Mia Hamm · Bill Clinton · Joan of Arc · Billie Holiday · Al Capone ·
csso · Jane Austen · Muhammad Ali · Mohandas Gandhi · Orson Welles ·
ntez · John Wilkes Booth · Yury Gagarin · Jackie Robinson · Anne Bo
arriet Tubman · Ludwig van Beethoven · Babe Ruth · Thomas Jeffers
rtin Luther King Jr. · Lou Gehrig · Jeannette Rankin · Michelangelo ·
mstrong · Amelia Earhart · Ferdinand Magellan · Harriet Beecher St
hristopher Reeve · James Cook · Sir Isaac Newton · Henry Ford · A
tchinson · Vladimir Ilyich Lenin · Theodore Roosevelt · Karl Marx · J
esar · Leonardo da Vinci · Jimmy Carter · Dwight D. Eisenhowe
een Liliuokalani · Rachel Carson · George Washington · Geronin
arlemagne · Clara Barton · Richard Nixon · Benito Mussolini · Al

introduction

We've all heard it. Some of us have even said it.
The eternal whine of one generation to the next:

When I was your age...
...I walked ten miles through five feet of snow
to deliver newspapers.
...I had my own business and fifty employees.
...I worked my way around the world on a tramp steamer.

Whatever.

Regardless of the truth behind such claims, the point is always the same. At any given age, someone else accomplished a lot more than you have at the same age.

I was reminded of this on a recent birthday when I realized that I was now the same age as Robert E. Lee when he led the Army of Northern Virginia to disaster at Gettysburg. Here I was, my beard as gray as Lee's, and I hadn't even led a small army to a minor defeat! I'd done so little in my life!

Of course, when we use the lives of others as measuring sticks for our own, we are bound to come up short. As satirist Tom Lehrer once put it, "It is sobering to realize that when he was my age, Mozart had been dead for three years."

What follows is a compilation of the deeds performed at every age from four to ninety by someone great or notorious. Their achievements are guaranteed to make you feel small, unproductive, and inconsequential, if you don't already.

Still, I believe there is some value in such a compendium, beyond the meager joys of masochism. By examining the lives of others we can, perhaps, learn something about our own lives and life in general. We can see that each life has its own unique arc, and that success at one age may auger failure at another, or vice versa. Some lives peak early, then follow a steady downhill trend. Other lives blossom late (Grandma Moses). And a few favored individuals (Pablo Picasso, Tiger Woods) started out auspiciously and then went on to even greater triumphs. You never know.

So take heart. It's never too late (or too early) to do something grand and noteworthy. Or really stupid.

Happy birthday.

The research for this book was done mostly on the Internet, as well as in various books and encyclopedias. There is no bibliography because it would have been longer than the text. However, if you are interested in learning more about the lives of those mentioned here, a wealth of information is only a couple of mouse clicks away.

At Age 4...

Louis XIV became the king of France.

He didn't do much actual ruling at that age and was not officially crowned until 1654. The real ruler was Cardinal Mazarin until his death in 1661, when Louis (Sept. 15, 1638–Sept. 1, 1715) took personal charge. Altogether, he ruled France for seventy-two years— the longest reign of any European monarch. The son of Louis XIII and Anne of Austria, he was apparently neglected as a child; once he nearly drowned in a garden pond when his tenders were not paying attention. As king, Louis XIV was everything a proper king ought to be and was known as the Sun King because his brilliance outshone everyone else in seventeenth century Europe. He promoted arts and culture and built France into the continental superpower of the era, although in later years his habit of getting into unnecessary wars did his nation more harm than good. His most impressive achievement was turning what was once a small hunting lodge into the magnificent palace at Versailles, which was completed in 1695.

At Age 5...

Wolfgang Amadeus Mozart produced his first musical composition.

Mozart

It was six measures long, andante, and in the key of C major. Young Wolfgang (Jan. 27, 1756–Dec. 5, 1791) gave his first concert at age six and embarked on his first concert tour at age seven. By the time Mozart was nine, his father—Leopold, a court musician—was lying about his son's age, trimming a year from the young prodigy's actual age in order to attract larger audiences. Like stage parents of a later era, Leopold devoted himself totally to promoting his son's career. "We are being talked of everywhere," he wrote. "Everyone is amazed…and everyone whom I have heard says that his genius is incomprehensible." That much, at least, was true. Although he died young, Mozart is credited with having produced at least 626 compositions, including some of the greatest works of Western music. Aside from his music, today he is known mainly from the film *Amadeus*, which portrayed him as a giggling, self-indulgent, Enlightenment rock star. The movie was more fiction than fact, yet it did get at a deeper truth. To his rival, Salieri, and to all of us, Mozart's genius truly was incomprehensible.

At Age 6...

Shirley Temple became Hollywood's number one box-office star.

With films such as *Stand up and Cheer*, *Little Miss Marker*, and *Wee Willie Winkle*, she remained the most popular movie star from 1934 through 1937. Depression-era audiences just couldn't get enough of Shirley (b. Apr. 23, 1928) as the pint-sized package of bubbly talent sang, danced, and smiled her way into America's collective heart. Almost single-handedly, she rescued the Fox studio from bankruptcy. She continued her career as she made the difficult transition from child star to ingénue, but in 1949, at the ripe old age of twenty-one, she retired from acting. She returned to the public eye twenty years later when, as Shirley Temple Black, she was named a U.S. delegate to the United Nations. Later, she served as the American ambassador to Ghana (1974) and the Czech Republic (1989). A breast cancer survivor and the author of two well-received autobiographies, she recently said, "If I had to do it all over again, I wouldn't change anything."

At Age 7...

William Bligh went to sea for the first time.

Remembered today mainly as the sadistic captain of the HMS Bounty, Bligh (Sept. 9, 1754–Dec. 17, 1817) has gotten a bad rap from history—or, at least, from Hollywood. Bligh was actually no more brutal than a typical Royal Navy captain of that era. After his first voyage as a personal servant to the captain of HMS Monmouth, Bligh joined the Royal Navy in 1770. Given command of the Bounty in 1787 at age thirty-three, his mission was to sail to Tahiti and secure samples of breadfruit. The famous mutiny in April 1789 probably had less to do with Bligh's presumed cruelty than with his crew's desire to return to the paradise of Tahiti. The mutineers put Bligh adrift in a twenty-three-foot open boat with eighteen other men. In what is regarded as one of the greatest feats of seamanship on record, Bligh sailed 3,618 miles in forty-seven days, safely reaching the Dutch port of Java. Upon his return to England, naval authorities absolved him of any blame in the mutiny. In 1805, he was appointed governor of the penal colony at New South Wales, Australia, only to face another mutiny—the so-called Rum Rebellion, sparked by his attempt to end the use of rum as currency; he again was held blameless. He died at age sixty-three, in 1817, with the rank of Rear Admiral.

At Age 8...

Tiger Woods won his first international golf tournament.

A golfing phenomenon from the age of two, when he appeared on The Mike Douglas Show, Tiger (b. Dec. 30, 1975) has more than lived up to his early promise. Young Eldrick was nicknamed Tiger by his father, Earl, in honor of a Vietnam War buddy. Earl carefully tutored his son in linksmanship, and by 1984, at age eight, Tiger won the first of six consecutive Optimist International Junior World titles. From 1991 through 1996, he won three consecutive U.S. Junior Amateur titles, followed by three straight U.S. Amateur titles. Turning professional in 1996 at the age of twenty, he won two of his first eight tournaments. The following year, he became the youngest ever winner of the prestigious Masters Tournament. His greatest achievement (so far) came in 2000, when he won three Major tournaments, including the U.S. Open and British Open, both by record margins. After winning his ninth and tenth Major titles in 2005, Tiger, at age thirty, was more than halfway to his stated goal of eclipsing Jack Nicklaus's record of eighteen Major championships. In 2004, he married a beautiful Swedish model. He's also richer than God. Not bad, Tiger.

At Age 9...

Michael Jackson had his first hit record.

The seventh of nine children in a musical family, the "Gloved One" (b. Aug. 29, 1958) became lead singer of The Jackson Five when he was only five. The group signed with Motown Records in 1968, and their first release, "I Want You Back," quickly rose to the top of the charts, as did their next three records. Going solo, in 1982 Jackson recorded *Thriller*, the number-one album of all time, with more than fifty million sales worldwide. At about that time, it became apparent that the moonwalking superstar was a little, well...unusual. He went through a series of publicly denied but blatantly obvious plastic surgeries. There were bizarre rumors about what went on at his famed Neverland ranch. And finally...criminal charges of child molestation. Although he was acquitted of all charges in a headline-making trial in 2005, many questions remained. It all left a generation of fans wondering whatever became of that cute, talented little kid who used to sing with The Jackson Five.

At Age 10...

Ethelred the Unready became king of England.

In the year 978, Ethelred II (968?–1016) became king following the murder of his half-brother, Edward the Martyr—a plot in which young Ethelred may have been implicated. At the time, England was under constant assault by Viking raiders from Denmark. In an attempt to buy off the Vikings, Ethelred began collecting a tax known as the Danegeld. That made him unpopular with his subjects, so he tried a new approach: in 1002, he initiated a series of massacres of Danish colonists. That made him even less popular with the Danes, who responded with renewed attacks that forced Ethelred to flee to Normandy in 1013. He returned the following year, and died in London in 1016. His sobriquet is more correctly Ethelred the Unræd, an Old English word meaning badly advised or unwise. That was certainly true.

At Age 11...

Elvis Presley got a
guitar for his birthday.

That turned out to have been a pretty good investment. Elvis (Jan. 8, 1935–Aug. 16, 1977) made his first recordings in the summer of 1953, at age eighteen. By 1955, he was appearing on local Memphis TV shows and made his national debut in 1956 on the Dorsey Brothers show. His raw energy and hip-waggling stage presence soon made Elvis the Pelvis the first rock 'n' roll superstar. Drafted into the army in 1958, he returned in 1960, his career carefully managed by "Colonel" Tom Parker. Throughout the sixties, he made a series of pleasant but forgettable movies and churned out commercially successful records that somehow lacked the dangerous sexuality that had made him a star in the fifties. By the late sixties, rock 'n' roll had passed him by, and he became a virtual recluse in his Graceland mansion, surrounded by his Memphis Mafia. But he made a comeback in the seventies, fueled by his appearances in Las Vegas. He died at forty-two, a victim of drug habits and a weak heart. A quarter-century after his death, he is perhaps more popular than ever, and each year thousands of his devoted fans make a pilgrimage to Graceland to honor the King.

At Age 12...

Ernest Hemingway got
his first shotgun.

In literature, this is known as foreshadowing. The shotgun—a single-barreled 20-gauge—was a gift from his father, a doctor who committed suicide by gunshot in 1928. Hemingway (July 21, 1899–July 2, 1961) began his writing career at seventeen as a newspaper reporter. He went to Europe as an ambulance driver in World War I and adopted a bohemian, expatriate lifestyle in postwar Paris. These experiences provided the background for his first successful novel, The Sun Also Rises (1925). His lean, distinctive writing style influenced a generation of writers, and many of his works—A Farewell to Arms, For Whom the Bell Tolls, The Old Man and the Sea—are regarded as modern classics. Hemingway's real life was at least as tumultuous as anything in his novels, and his talent, oversized ego, and brazen exploits made him something of a living legend. It was a reputation he coveted and consciously shaped. He won the Nobel Prize for Literature in 1954. But by the late fifties, illness and the effects of his frequent injuries had robbed him of his energy and willpower. Unable to hunt, fish, or even write, Hemingway put a double-barreled shotgun to his head and ended his remarkable life at age sixty-one.

At Age 13...

Bill Gates learned to
program a computer.

In the late sixties, computers were big, complex, expensive devices that could be found only in business offices, universities, and large institutions. No one had a personal computer, because they didn't exist. But young William Henry Gates (b. Oct. 28, 1955) was fascinated by computers and had a vision for the future. He enrolled at Harvard, but dropped out in his junior year and founded Microsoft with his childhood friend, Paul Allen, in 1975. Seemingly the ultimate computer nerd, Gates was actually a shrewd businessman, and soon secured the right to produce the software operating system (MS-DOS) for IBM's new line of personal computers. In the eighties, as computers made their way into millions of homes, Microsoft became to the software industry what Standard Oil had been to the petroleum industry a century earlier—a virtual monopoly. And the still-youthful computer nerd became the richest man on the planet, with a fortune estimated at around $40 billion. A generous and creative philanthropist, Gates and his wife, Melinda, have devoted themselves to supporting worthwhile causes around the world.

At Age 14...

Buffalo Bill Cody joined the Pony Express.

Born in Iowa, William Frederick Cody (Feb. 16, 1846–Jan. 10, 1917) became a rider for the short-lived Pony Express in Julesburg, Colorado. Like Cody, most Pony Express riders were slightly built teenagers, in order to lighten the load on the horses. The telegraph soon made the Pony Express obsolete, so Cody turned to hunting buffalo to supply the army. By the age of twenty-two, his skill in that line of work had won him the nickname of Buffalo Bill. In 1876, just three weeks after the battle of Little Bighorn, Cody killed and scalped a Cheyenne warrior, shouting, "First scalp for Custer!" He started his famed Wild West Show in 1882 and soon became a star of international renown; he was probably the most famous American in the late nineteenth century. His show played before the crowned heads of Europe (Queen Victoria enjoyed it) and featured the likes of Annie Oakley, Wild Bill Hickock, and the Sioux chief, Sitting Bull. Perhaps feeling guilty about some of his earlier exploits, he became an advocate for Native American rights and conservation. He also supported equal rights for women. Unfortunately, due to a series of bad investments, he was nearly broke when he died at the age of seventy.

At Age 15...

Mia Hamm joined
the U.S. National
Soccer Team.

Mia Hamm (b. March 17, 1972) hit the big time at fifteen and stayed there—for a record seventeen years. The youngest player ever to make the national team, Hamm played for her junior high school's football team but wisely decided to concentrate on soccer. She attended the University of North Carolina and led the Tar Heels to four consecutive NCAA titles. In 1991, Hamm's U.S. team won the FIFA Women's World Cup; at nineteen, she was the youngest-ever member of a winning team. After taking the gold medal in the 1996 Olympics, the team won another FIFA World Cup title in 1999 in a dramatic game played before ninety thousand fans in the Rose Bowl—the largest crowd ever to see a women's sporting event. In 2004, Hamm married baseball star Nomar Garciaparra, and announced her retirement from soccer following another Olympic gold medal. In the course of her stellar career, she scored 158 goals in international competition, more than any other player—male or female—in the history of the sport.

At Age 16...

Bill Clinton shook
JFK's hand.

T he encounter on the White House lawn was filmed for posterity, and inspired William Jefferson Blythe Clinton (b. Aug. 19, 1946) to seek a life in public service. After attending Yale Law School and winning a Rhodes scholarship, Clinton in 1978 became the youthful governor of Arkansas and, in 1993, the forty-second President of the United States. In two controversial terms, Clinton presided over the longest unbroken period of peace and prosperity in American history. He reformed the welfare system, reduced inflation and unemployment, and produced the first balanced federal budget since the administration of Andrew Jackson. He also showed incredibly bad judgment in his personal affairs. In that, he followed too closely in the footsteps of John F. Kennedy, the idol of his youth. Perhaps the difference between Kennedy and Clinton is reflected in the difference between Marilyn Monroe and Monica Lewinsky. Even in his misdeeds, JFK at least had a touch of class.

At Age 17...

Sacagawea joined
the Lewis and Clark
expedition.

The young Shoshone woman (1788?–1812) was kidnapped by a party of Hidatsa at age twelve, and by 1805 she had been purchased and married by the French trapper, Charbonneau. While wintering at the Mandan village in North Dakota, they met Lewis and Clark, who hired Charbonneau as a guide and translator. Charbonneau proved to be virtually worthless, but Sacagawea turned out to be an important asset to the expedition. She was not really a guide, since most of the time they traveled through territory she had never seen, but her mere presence in the party convinced Indians they encountered that they were not hostile, since women were never taken along on war parties. Shortly before leaving the Mandan village, Sacagawea—whose name meant "bird woman"—gave birth to a son, Jean Baptiste, nicknamed Pompey by the explorers. She and her child accompanied the expedition all the way to the Pacific and back. Although some stories suggest that she lived to be nearly one hundred and died in 1884, that is probably a case of mistaken identity. There is good evidence that the real Sacagawea died of a fever in 1812.

At Age 18...

Billie Holiday made her
first recording.

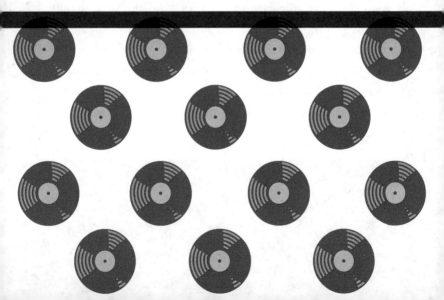

Born to a thirteen-year-old prostitute and a fifteen-year-old jazz guitarist, Eleanora Holiday (Apr. 7, 1915–July 17, 1959) survived a difficult childhood in Baltimore and began singing in Harlem nightclubs in the early 1930s. There, she was discovered by record producer John Hammond, who arranged for her first recording session in 1933—of an otherwise forgettable song called "Your Mother's Son-in-Law." Billie debuted at the famed Apollo Theater in November 1934, and was an immediate hit. As a singer her range was very limited, but her phrasing, timing, and emotions made her a blues legend. As she said of one of her down-and-dirty ditties, "I've lived songs like that." And, indeed, her life imitated her art. By the 1940s she was addicted to heroin, and she endured a series of abusive marriages and relationships, the last to a Mafia enforcer. In and out of jails and hospitals, by the fifties she had lost her New York cabaret license, making it impossible for her to perform there. She died of cirrhosis of the liver at forty-five, leaving behind a tragic legend and her enduring signature songs, "God Bless the Child" and the anti-lynching classic, "Strange Fruit."

At Age 19...

Al Capone was arrested
for the first time—for
disorderly conduct.

The man who would become the best-known criminal in American history began his career as a bouncer in the Brooklyn speakeasy of crime boss Frankie Yale. It was while working there that Alphonse Capone (Jan. 17, 1899–Jan. 25, 1947) acquired the scar that gave him his nickname— Scarface. When Capone made an unwelcome remark to young Lena Galluchio ("You've got a nice ass, and I mean that as a compliment!"), her brother, small-time gangster Frank Galluchio, went after him with a knife. The dispute was smoothed over, and eventually Galluchio went to work for Capone. By 1923, Capone had moved on to Chicago, where he vied for control of the Windy City's rackets with George "Bugs" Moran. At Capone's order, six of Moran's men, plus an unlucky friend, were gunned down in the infamous St. Valentine's Day Massacre in 1929; Moran was across the street at the time, while Capone, innocently enough, was at his home in Florida. Capone was never arrested for any of the many murders that were committed at his behest, nor for the bootlegging and rum-running operations that made him a millionaire many times over. But he made a fatal mistake in failing to give the government a piece of his action; in 1931 Capone was finally convicted of income tax evasion. Sentenced to ten years, he quickly took over the Atlanta federal pen, so he was transferred to Alcatraz, where he became a model prisoner. Released in 1939 and suffering from syphilitic dementia, Capone died in Florida at age 48.

At Age 20...

Leif Ericsson established the first European colony in North America.

Around the year AD 1000, Leif Ericsson (980?–1020?), the son of Eric the Red, sailed west from Greenland with a crew of about thirty-five. Moving southward along the coasts of Baffin Island and Labrador, they established a base camp at L'Anse aux Meadows on the northeast coast of Newfoundland (the camp was discovered by archeologists in 1961). Leif hoped to found a permanent colony that would become a source of timber, which was in short supply at the Norse colonies in Greenland. However, the Viking colonists immediately ran into trouble with the natives, whom they called "skraelings." In their first encounter, the Vikings killed eight of the skraelings, who responded with an attack on the base camp in which Thorvald, another son of Eric the Red, was killed. The colony survived for about ten years and then was abandoned, probably due to the continued hostility of the skraelings. It was another six centuries before Europeans again attempted to establish permanent settlements along the shoreline of North America.

At Age 21...

Jane Austen got her first rejection slip.

J ane Austen (Dec. 16, 1775–July 18, 1817) began her writing career at about age twelve—when she wasn't busy playing games, including, curiously enough, an early English form of baseball. She began writing novels at nineteen, but her first completed work, *Pride and Prejudice*, was turned down in 1797 by a publisher who declined to look at it. She finally made her first sale in 1803 when she received ten pounds for *Northanger Abbey*. However, the publisher changed his mind and didn't print it; the book was published at long last fourteen years later, after Austen's death. Her first published novel was *Sense and Sensibility*, which she published anonymously and "at her own risk" in 1811, at age thirty-five. Eventually, she made 140 pounds on it. All her novels were closely observed studies of human nature and revealed a keen wit. Jane never married, although she was described by an acquaintance as "the prettiest, silliest, most affected husband-hunting butterfly." She died in 1817, probably of Addison's Disease, at age forty-one.

At Age 22...

Muhammad Ali won his first heavyweight title.

Cassius Marcellus Clay (b. Jan. 17, 1942) was born in Louisville, Kentucky. The young Clay won the Olympic light-heavyweight Gold Medal at Rome in 1960. Turning pro and moving up to the heavyweight class, in 1964 he fought the reigning champ, the glowering Charles "Sonny" Liston. With his unparalleled combination of size, speed, and power, Clay made mincemeat of Liston, who failed to answer the bell for the seventh round. Clay bounded around the ring, shouting, "I am the greatest!" And he was. When his controversial career ended in 1981, he had won the title twice more and retired with a record of fifty-six wins (thirty-seven by KO) and five losses. By then, he was Muhammad Ali, devout Muslim and possibly the most famous man in the world. In several end-of-the-century polls, he was selected as the greatest athlete of the twentieth century. He was said to "float like a butterfly and sting like a bee." His courageous battle against Parkinson's disease has won the admiration even of many who resented him for his resistance to the draft in the late sixties. Love him or hate him, you could never ignore Muhammad Ali.

At Age 23...

Mohandas Gandhi was kicked off a train in South Africa.

As a London-educated lawyer wearing a dapper Western-style business suit, in June 1893 the young Gandhi (Oct. 2, 1869–Jan. 30, 1948) confidently bought a first-class ticket on a train in Pietermaritzburg, South Africa. He was promptly booted off the train, bag and baggage, for his effrontery; he was not white and therefore, by definition, not entitled to first-class status in anything. With that unceremonious beginning, Gandhi began a lifetime of activism that would ultimately cost the British Empire the jewel in its crown: India. After several years of legal battles in South Africa on behalf of the Indian people living there, Gandhi returned home to India and adopted the garb of a simple peasant. Through a series of massive demonstrations, imprisonments, and hunger strikes, Gandhi achieved world fame and popular support in India that bordered on religious idolatry. The mighty British Empire simply could not withstand Gandhi's determined campaign to win independence for India. His tactic of civil disobedience and nonviolent resistance proved to be a weapon against which the British could not maintain a defense. India achieved independence in 1947 but quickly fell into a civil war between Hindus and Muslims, resulting in the partitioning of the subcontinent into the separate states of India and Pakistan. Gandhi was assassinated by a religious zealot on January 30, 1948.

At Age 24...

Charlie Chaplin, Orson Welles, and Steven Spielberg all made their first movies.

Charlie Chaplin (Apr. 16, 1889–Dec. 25, 1977) began his show business career at age five, performing with his parents in London music halls. He came to America in 1910, at twenty-one, as a Vaudeville performer. He went to Hollywood in 1913 to make his first movie, a two-reeler called *Making a Living*, in which he played a small-time swindler posing as a newspaper reporter. In his next film, *Kid Auto Races at Venice*, Chaplin introduced his immortal character, The Little Tramp, complete with baggy pants (borrowed from Fatty Arbuckle) and oversized shoes. He made thirty-five films in 1914 and soon began directing, as well as starring in, his own films. By 1917, he was the most popular movie star in the world. He survived the transition to sound, making such classics as *City Lights*, *Modern Times*, and *The Great Dictator*. Tax problems, personal scandals, and political incorrectness drove him from the United States in 1952, and he spent the rest of his life living in Switzerland. He made his last film, *A Countess from Hong Kong*, in 1967, starring with Marlon Brando and Sophia Loren; it proved to be his only box office failure.

At Age 25...

Lola Montez became
the power behind the
throne of Bavaria.

The origins of this legendary temptress (Feb. 17, 1821?–Jan. 17, 1861) are obscure. Most sources say she was born in Ireland as Eliza Rosanna Gilbert, the daughter of a British officer and a beautiful Spanish woman. Other sources say she was born as early as 1818, the illegitimate daughter of an Irish parliamentarian. She spent her early years in India and Scotland, and at a boarding school in Bath, England, before running off at age sixteen to marry army officer Lt. Charles James. When he left her, Mrs. James reinvented herself as Lola Montez, exotic dancer. She opened on the London stage in 1843, performing her sensuous "Tarantula Dance." Alas, she was, it seems, a terrible dancer and was hooted off the stage after being recognized as plain old Mrs. James. She then floated around Europe, dancing and romancing; she is said to have had affairs with Alexander Dumas and Franz Liszt. In 1846, when she was fired by the manager of a Munich theater, she marched into the private study of an astonished and bedazzled King Ludwig to protest her treatment. In short order, the theater manager was fired, and Lola was the new mistress of "Mad King Ludwig." A year later, she was named Countess of Landsfeld; she is said to have coined the phrase, "Whatever Lola wants, Lola gets." She wanted power and got far too much of it to please Metternich and the Bavarian conservatives, who opposed the whip-carrying beauty. Student riots erupted (both pro- and anti-Lola) in 1848, forcing Ludwig to abdicate and Lola to flee. She roamed the world, performing in Australia and the California gold fields, making a living from her scandalous reputation and atrocious dancing. She died of pneumonia in New York City in 1861, shortly before her fortieth birthday.

At Age 26...

John Wilkes Booth
assassinated Abraham
Lincoln.

The illegitimate son of English actor Junius Booth, the future assassin began his own stage career in Philadelphia, receiving mediocre reviews. Booth (May 10, 1838–Apr. 26, 1865) moved to Richmond in 1858 at age twenty, and found that he liked the Southern lifestyle. He joined a Virginia militia unit just so he could watch the hanging of abolitionist John Brown. His acting career took off, and he was soon making a princely twenty thousand dollars a year. He dabbled briefly in Pennsylvania oil before taking up plotting against the government as his main avocation. Leading a motley band of conspirators, Booth shot Lincoln in the back of the head with a .44 caliber Deringer at Ford's Theater on April 14, 1865, just a week after Lee's surrender at Appomattox. Escaping from Washington, he was cornered in a barn in northern Virginia, where he was fatally shot in the neck. Staring at his paralyzed hands, his last words were, "Useless, useless." Found on his body were photographs of his fiancée and four other pretty girls.

At Age 27...

Marilyn Monroe
married Joe DiMaggio.

It was a marriage seemingly made in a publicist's heaven—the Yankee Clipper and Hollywood's greatest sex symbol. Marilyn (June 1, 1926–Aug. 5, 1962) and Joe tied the knot on January 14, 1954; by that fall they had separated. DiMaggio wanted a stay-at-home housewife, while Marilyn wanted to be Marilyn Monroe. But being Marilyn Monroe was never easy. She tried to counter her image as a lightweight sexpot by going east to study acting with Lee Strasberg and, not incidentally, by marrying playwright Arthur Miller. In Billy Wilder's *Some Like It Hot*, she finally proved her talent as an actress, but her marriage to Miller faltered and her drinking and pill-popping began to take a toll on her. She had a brief affair with President John F. Kennedy, but by the summer of 1962 she was seriously considering another marriage with DiMaggio. On the night of August 5, 1962, she was found dead from an apparent drug overdose. Conspiracy theorists have raised many questions about her death, but it will probably never be known whether it was suicide, murder, or simply a tragic accident.

At Age 28...

Jackie Robinson
was named
Rookie of the Year.

J ack Roosevelt Robinson (Jan. 31, 1919–Oct. 24, 1972) became the National League Rookie of the Year in 1947, but arguably he was the most important Major League rookie of any year. When, following World War II, Brooklyn Dodgers president Branch Rickey decided the time had come to break baseball's color line and sign an African-American ballplayer, he chose Robinson for the role. Intelligent, fierce, and talented, Robinson was asked by Rickey to have the courage "not to fight back" for the first two years. Despite enormous provocation and abuse, Robinson kept his word to Rickey and avoided the sort of on-field altercations that might have forced an end to the experiment. But there was nothing restrained about the way Jackie played the game; his determination, skills, and especially his speed quickly made him one of the dominant players in the National League. In 1949, he won the Most Valuable Player Award. Despite a short career (he retired in 1957) he was elected to the Hall of Fame in 1962. Robinson's contributions to both baseball and the civil rights revolution of the fifties and sixties cannot be overstated. In 1997, the fiftieth anniversary of his rookie year, Major League Baseball recognized Robinson's unique place in history by retiring his number, 42; no big league player will ever wear it again.

At Age 29...

Anne Boleyn
lost her head.

King Henry VIII probably first noticed Anne Boleyn (1507?–May 19, 1536) around 1522 when she became an attendant to his wife, Catherine of Aragon. Well-educated, intelligent, and vivacious (although no great beauty—she was said to have had a sixth finger on her left hand), Anne watched and waited as political intrigue swirled around the king and his queen. Although popular with the masses, Catherine had failed to bear a son and heir for Henry. When Henry sought to end his marriage, he ran afoul of the Catholic Church, and eventually broke with Rome over the issue. In the meantime, he courted Anne, who remained aloof as long as possible. But Henry's intentions were obvious, and at one point eight thousand of Catherine's supporters marched through the streets intending to lynch Anne. Finally, in 1533, Henry declared his marriage to Catherine invalid and wed Anne. She soon bore him a daughter, who would become Elizabeth I, but no sons. Henry's eye began to rove toward Jane Seymour, and he wanted to be rid of his strong-willed wife. In 1536, Anne was charged with witchcraft, incest, and adultery. She was beheaded in the Tower of London on May 19, 1536. On May 30, Henry married Jane Seymour.

At Age 30...

Harriet Tubman became a conductor on the Underground Railroad.

Born a slave in Maryland, Harriet (1820?–Mar. 10, 1913) married John Tubman, a free black man, in 1844. Fearing that she would be sold, she urged John to flee with her, but he elected to remain in Maryland while Harriet successfully escaped to Philadelphia in 1849. There, she became active in the Anti-Slavery Society, and in 1850 made her first trip south as a conductor on the Underground Railroad. In all, she made nineteen such trips, successfully conveying more than three hundred slaves, including her own mother and father, to freedom in Canada. Although for several years Harriet attempted to convince John Tubman to join her, they remained separated until his death in 1867. She boasted that she never lost a "passenger" and said, "If I could have convinced more slaves that they were slaves, I could have freed thousands more." Despite a forty-thousand-dollar bounty on her head, Tubman fearlessly pursued her work and evaded capture. She was a tough, no-nonsense leader, and informed runaway slaves that if they changed their minds, they would be shot, because "dead men tell no tales." Abolitionist John Brown called her "General Tubman" and said she was "one of the bravest persons on the continent." During the Civil War, she served the Union Army as a spy. She remarried following the war and lived quietly in New York State until her death in 1913 at age ninety-three.

At Age 31...

Ludwig van Beethoven realized that he was going deaf.

Like Mozart, Beethoven (Dec. 17, 1770–March 27, 1827) was the son of a court musician who attempted to present him—without much success in this case—as a child prodigy. Moving to Vienna in 1792, Beethoven studied with Joseph Haydn and soon became known as a piano virtuoso. He began composing piano concertos such as "Moonlight" Sonata (1801), and then full symphonies. But in 1802, Beethoven noticed that his ability to hear was fading. Depressed by the realization, he contemplated suicide, but managed to rally and entered a period of remarkable productivity. He composed his famous Fifth Symphony in 1807–08, at age thirty-eight. To many critics, the heroic tones of this work and others resonate with Beethoven's personal struggle against his advancing deafness. He was a quarrelsome, troubled man who never married. He stopped composing in 1826 and died at age fifty-six the following year, probably of liver disease.

At Age 32...

Babe Ruth hit sixty home runs in a season.

George Herman Ruth (Feb. 6, 1895–Aug. 16, 1948) was an all-American character who could have been invented by Mark Twain. A boisterous and delinquent child, he was sent to a Catholic reform school in Baltimore, where he learned to play baseball. Signed by the Boston Red Sox in 1914, the young Babe became one of the best pitchers in the game. He could also hit a little. It became apparent that he would be more valuable as an everyday player than as a pitcher, so by 1919 he became a regular outfielder. That year, he swatted a record twenty-nine home runs. After the season, Boston owner Harry Frazee, in need of cash to finance his Broadway production of No, No, Nanette, sold Ruth to the New York Yankees—thus inaugurating the "Curse of the Bambino" that haunted Boston until the Sox finally won the World Series again in 2004. In New York, Ruth became a sensation, with fifty-nine homers in 1921. He bested that in 1927 with sixty, a record that stood for thirty-four years. He was known for his gargantuan appetite—supposedly for hot dogs and soda pop. In reality, the Babe's appetites were more adult, and he was a familiar figure in Prohibition era speakeasies and brothels. In 1934, his talent fading, he was released by the Yankees and signed with the Boston Braves. On May 25, 1935, he provided one last hurrah by clouting three homers in a game at Pittsburgh. A week later, he retired with a lifetime total of 714 home runs, a record that lasted until Hank Aaron broke it in 1974. The Babe, who is still considered the greatest baseball player of all time, died of throat cancer in 1948, at the age of fifty-three.

At Age 33...

Thomas Jefferson
wrote the Declaration
of Independence.

As a young and relatively obscure Virginia delegate to the Continental Congress in 1776, Jefferson (Apr. 13, 1743–July 4, 1826) was appointed to the committee designated to draft the Declaration of Independence. He did most of the writing, but not everything he wrote made it into the final version. Specifically, he included a paragraph condemning King George III for inflicting the slave trade upon the colonies. The paragraph was deleted, so as not to offend the Southern colonies. But Jefferson, although a slave owner himself, knew that slavery was wrong and must someday end. "I tremble for my nation," he said, "when I consider that God is just." Yet he could never bring himself to free his own slaves, without whom he could not have lived the kind of life he preferred; the shackles of the slavery system bound master as well as servant. High-minded in great matters but weak in his personal life, Jefferson embodied the contradictions inherent in the American experiment in self-government. However, his achievements as patriot, president, scientist, and philosopher are beyond dispute. Jefferson died on July 4, 1826, the fiftieth anniversary of the Declaration, and the same day as his friend and rival, John Adams.

At Age 34...

Martin Luther King Jr.
gave his
"I have a dream"
speech.

One of the most important figures in American history, King (Jan. 15, 1929–Apr. 4, 1968) fought for racial equality and challenged white America to live up to Jefferson's assertion that "all men are created equal." He rose to national prominence in 1955 as a leader in the Montgomery, Alabama, bus boycott, which was sparked by Rosa Parks's refusal to give up her seat on a public bus. As head of the Southern Christian Leadership Council, King traveled over six million miles and gave more than two thousand speeches, none more important than the one he delivered at the Lincoln Memorial on August 28, 1963, before a crowd of two hundred and fifty thousand. With soaring rhetoric and passionate conviction, King spoke of a day when people would be judged by "the content of their character," rather than by the color of their skin. A disciple of Thoreau and Gandhi, he preached nonviolent resistance in the face of intolerable persecution: his house was bombed, he was assaulted at least four times, and he was arrested more than twenty times. In 1964, he became the youngest person ever to win the Nobel Peace Prize. He was assassinated in Memphis, Tennessee, on April 4, 1968, at the age of thirty-nine. Today, his birthday is a national holiday.

At Age 35...

Lou Gehrig
took himself out
of the lineup.

The son of German immigrants, Henry Louis Gehrig (June 19, 1903–June 2, 1941) was born in Manhattan, attended Columbia University, and, in 1923, signed with the New York Yankees. A left-handed first baseman, Gehrig pinch-hit for Pee Wee Wanninger on June 1, 1925. The next day, regular first baseman Wally Pipp had a minor injury in batting practice, so Gehrig started in his place. Pipp never got his job back. Hitting for power and a high batting average, Gehrig joined teammate Babe Ruth in the heart of the Yankee "Murderers' Row" batting order. He won the Most Valuable Player Award in 1927 and 1936. For those who see good chemistry as a key to winning baseball, it is worth noting that Gehrig and Ruth—polar opposites in personality—despised one another. Gehrig became known as "The Iron Horse," as year after year he played through injuries and never missed a game. But as the 1939 season began, it became apparent that Gehrig's skills had suddenly vanished, and he could barely make even routine plays. Finally, on May 2, 1939, after playing 2,130 consecutive games (a record eventually eclipsed by Cal Ripken Jr. in 1995), Gehrig took himself out of the lineup. It was soon discovered that Gehrig was suffering from a degenerative muscle disease, amyotropic lateral sclerosis, or ALS—now commonly known as Lou Gehrig's disease. After an emotional farewell at Yankee Stadium, during which he declared himself "the luckiest man on the face of the earth," Gehrig died on June 2, 1941, at the age of thirty-seven.

At Age 36...

Jeannette Rankin became the first woman elected to Congress.

Born on the frontier in Missoula, Montana, Jeannette Rankin (June 11, 1880–May 18, 1973) graduated from Montana University in 1902 and spent several years working as a teacher and social worker. An activist in the women's suffrage movement, she ran for Congress from Montana in 1916, four years before women won the right to vote nationwide. She took office in 1917, the first woman ever to serve in the House of Representatives. A Republican, she joined fifty-six other representatives in voting against the declaration of war against Germany in World War I. In 1918, she tried, but failed, to win the Montana nomination to the U.S. Senate. She spent the next twenty years working as a peace activist and was again elected to Congress in 1940, on a peace platform. Following the Japanese attack on Pearl Harbor on December 7, 1941, she was the only member of Congress to vote against the declaration of war against Japan. Rankin explained that she didn't believe any nation should ever go to war unanimously. Her vote aroused considerable anger, and she had to be protected from vengeful mobs. She declined to run for reelection. Later, she traveled to India to study with the master of nonviolence, Mohandas Gandhi. In 1968, at the age of eighty-seven, she led five thousand women of the "Jeannette Rankin Brigade" in a Washington, D.C., protest against the war in Vietnam. In 1985, she was honored with a statue in the Capitol's National Statuary Hall.

At Age 37...

Michelangelo completed work on the ceiling of the Sistine Chapel.

Painter, sculptor, architect, and poet, Michelangelo di Lodovico Buonarotti Simoni (Mar. 6, 1475–Feb. 18, 1564) was perhaps the greatest of Renaissance artists. Spending most of his time in Florence and Rome, and initially sponsored by Lorenzo de' Medici, Michelangelo created early works mainly in the form of sculptures, including the famous statue David (1500). Pope Julius II commissioned Michelangelo to build his tomb but frequently diverted him to other projects, with the result that Michelangelo worked on the tomb for some forty years without ever finishing it. In 1508, Julius put Michelangelo to work on a fresco for the ceiling of the Vatican's Sistine Chapel. When the arduous task was completed in 1512, Michelangelo said, "After four tortured years, four hundred over-life-sized figures, I felt as old and weary as Jeremiah. I was only thirty-seven, yet friends did not recognize the old man I had become." Michelangelo lived another fifty-two years, completing many more great works of art, including the fresco of The Last Judgment and the architecture of St. Peter's Basilica.

At Age 38...

Neil Armstrong landed
on the moon.

A small-town boy from Wapokoneta, Ohio, Neil Alden Armstrong (b. Aug. 5, 1930) was educated at Purdue and the University of Southern California and served as a naval aviator from 1949 to 1952. He then became a civilian test pilot and a NASA astronaut. His first space flight, in *Gemini 8* (1966) with David Scott, was a near disaster, but cool work by Armstrong during a crisis resulted in a safe reentry. That earned him command of the *Apollo 11* mission to the moon, with Edwin (Buzz) Aldrin and Michael Collins. On July 20, 1969, Armstrong piloted the lunar module (LM) *Eagle* downward toward the cratered, rock-littered terrain of the Sea of Tranquility. With less than sixty seconds of fuel left, Armstrong found a clear area and smoothly set the *Eagle* down on the surface of the moon. Hours later, he made his way down the LM's ladder and became the first human to set foot on another world. "That's one small step for a man, one giant leap for mankind," Armstrong declared, in a statement worthy of the place in history it would be accorded. The three astronauts returned safely to Earth, but none of them ever flew in space again. Armstrong retired from NASA in 1971.

At Age 39...

Amelia Earhart
got lost.

A Kansas-born tomboy, Amelia Earhart (July 24, 1897–July 3, 1937?) became an aviation legend and the central figure in one of the twentieth century's greatest mysteries. She learned to fly in 1921, and a year later set a women's altitude record of 14,000 feet. In 1928, a year after Charles Lindbergh's historic first flight across the Atlantic, publisher and publicist George Putnam asked Amelia if she wanted to become the first woman to fly the Atlantic. She agreed, and on June 17, 1928, she was one of three people aboard a successful flight from Newfoundland to Wales. She was simply a passenger, but Putnam (whom she married in 1931) promoted her, to great acclaim, as the "Lady Lindy." In 1932, she tried a solo flight from Newfoundland to Paris but was forced to land in Ireland. In 1935, she became the first person to fly solo from Hawaii to Oakland, California. In 1937, she planned an around-the-world flight, but in her first attempt her Lockheed Electra crashed upon takeoff. With the plane repaired, she tried again, embarking with navigator Fred Noonan from Miami, on the 29,000-mile eastbound route. On July 2, they took off from Lae, New Guinea, on the most difficult leg of the trip, a 2,556-mile flight to tiny Howland Island in the Central Pacific. The following morning, Earhart and Noonan made radio contact with the Coast Guard cutter *Itasca*, reporting that they were running low on fuel and had not spotted Howland. When no further contact was made, a massive search was conducted, but was called off by July 19. Despite many theories, nothing more is known of the fate of Earhart and Noonan. Some claim that she was shot down by the Japanese and executed or imprisoned; it was even claimed that she survived and lived anonymously in New Jersey. Attempts to find the wreckage of the Electra continue but the mystery remains unsolved.

At Age 40...

Ferdinand Magellan
reached the straits that
bear his name.

Early in his life, Magellan (1480?–Apr. 27, 1521) took part in Portuguese expeditions to Africa and India, but when Portugal refused to support his plan for a westward voyage to the Spice Islands, he offered his services to the king of Spain. In 1519, he set out with a fleet of five ships but had to contend with disease and mutiny, as the other captains sought to seize command of the expedition. With some difficulty, Magellan managed to prevail, and in October 1520 he reached the head of the narrow, 373-mile-long passage at the tip of South America that is now known as the Strait of Magellan. After making his way through the dangerous waterway, he crossed the Pacific and arrived in the Philippines. There he was killed by unfriendly natives on the island of Mactan on April 27, 1521. His depleted fleet continued onward; of the five ships and 234 men who began the voyage, only one bedraggled vessel and eighteen scurvy-ridden men completed the first circumnavigation of the globe, returning to Spain in September 1522.

At Age 41...

Harriet Beecher Stowe
published
Uncle Tom's Cabin.

‘‘ So," said Abraham Lincoln upon meeting Harriet Beecher Stowe (June 14, 1811–July 1, 1896) in 1862, "you're the little woman who wrote the book that made this great war." Lincoln's comment was only a slight exaggeration. Harriet Beecher Stowe's novel *Uncle Tom's Cabin* is one of the most important books in American history and was a major contributing factor to the onset of the Civil War. The daughter of Calvinist preacher Lyman Beecher, Harriet lived for years in Cincinnati, where she came in contact with fugitive slaves from across the Ohio River in the slave state of Kentucky. She married Calvin E. Stowe, a professor at her father's college and had seven children. Her literary career began in 1834, and she began her great work as a series of installments in the antislavery journal, *National Era*, in 1851. It was published in book form in 1852 and within a year had sold some three million copies worldwide. The melodramatic and romanticized tale of the evils of slavery was denounced throughout the South, but won countless converts to abolitionism in the North. Stowe's novel put a personal face on slavery and inspired millions to make the eradication of the South's "peculiar institution" a moral imperative of the highest order. "Uncle Tom" later became a term of contempt among African Americans, mainly due to the blackface "Tom shows" that proliferated later in the century. But the Uncle Tom in Stowe's great novel is a noble, self-sacrificing, Christlike figure—and one of the most influential fictional characters of all time.

At Age 42...

Rosa Parks refused to give up her seat on a bus.

As an unknown African-American housewife, Rosa Parks (Feb. 4, 1913–Oct. 24, 2005) touched off the Civil Rights revolution on December 1, 1955, with a single act of defiance. The daughter of a carpenter and a teacher, Parks attended Alabama State Teachers College before settling in Montgomery with her husband, Raymond. She had been active in the local NAACP organization, but her historic act appears to have been a spur-of-the-moment decision. Tired after a long day of work, Parks refused to give up her seat on a city bus to a white person—a violation of Montgomery's segregation laws, for which she was arrested. The incident led to a 382-day boycott of city buses by Montgomery's large African-American community. One of the leaders in the boycott was a young local minister, Dr. Martin Luther King Jr. Eventually, the Supreme Court struck down the Montgomery ordinance, a landmark event on the road to equal rights for all Americans.

At Age 43...

James Cook found a
cure for scurvy.

The last of the great navigators of the Golden Age of Discovery, James Cook (Oct. 27, 1728–Feb. 14, 1779) was born into humble circumstances and began his seagoing career at the unusually late age of eighteen, when he took a job as a shipping company apprentice. After serving as captain of coal carriers on the North Sea, Cook joined the Royal Navy in 1755 at age twenty-seven. His talents as a navigator were soon recognized, and in 1768, at thirty-nine, he was appointed to lead an expedition to Tahiti to observe the transit of Venus across the face of the sun. During the course of the voyage of the Endeavor, Cook discovered New Zealand in 1769. On the return voyage in 1771, Cook experimented with feeding his crew fresh citrus fruit and sauerkraut as a means of avoiding the dread disease scurvy, the bane of long-distance explorers. The experiment was a success, and before long British sailors became known as "limeys," as Cook's remedy was applied throughout the British fleet. On his second voyage to the Pacific, Cook tried, but failed, to find evidence of a rumored southern continent; on his third voyage, in 1778, he did discover the Hawaiian Islands. Cook went on to explore the western coast of North America, returning to Hawaii in 1779, when he met his unfortunate fate. British arrogance and poor cross-cultural communication led to an incident with the natives, who killed Cook on the beach of Kealakekua Bay.

At Age 44...

Sir Isaac Newton published the *Principia*.

The son of a wealthy landowner who couldn't sign his own name and died three months before his son's birth, Newton (Jan. 4, 1642–Mar. 31, 1727) seems to have had a troubled youth: he once threatened to burn down the house of his mother and stepfather—with them in it. He entered Trinity College in Cambridge at eighteen and showed an early aptitude for mathematics. Working at home for two years because Cambridge was shut down due to the plague, Newton invented calculus and formulated his laws of motion before he was twenty-five. At twenty-seven, he was appointed Lucasian Professor at Cambridge. Following a nervous breakdown—he seems to have suffered from depression—he retired from active research in 1693 and spent the rest of his life working as a government official. In 1687, at forty-four, he published what is regarded as the greatest scientific treatise ever written, *Philosophiae naturalis principia mathematica*, known as the *Principia*. In it he elucidated, among other things, his theory of universal gravitation.

At Age 45...

Henry Ford introduced
the Model T.

B orn on a farm in Dearborn, Michigan, Ford (July 30, 1863–Apr. 7, 1947) showed an early interest in mechanical devices and found work as a machinist and engineer. By 1896, he had tinkered together his first automobile, the Quadricycle. He started the Ford Motor Company in 1903, and in 1908 he introduced the Model T. A decade later, half of all the cars in America were Model Ts. Ford pioneered assembly-line mass production, a technique that allowed him to keep the price of his automobiles low enough that they were afford-able to middle-class families. He also paid his workers well—six dollars a day—reasoning correctly that his workers were also potential customers. Nevertheless, Ford opposed the rise of labor unions, and he was the focus of violent clashes between labor and management in the thir-ties. Personally, Ford held some bizarre views and was responsible for the publication of a great deal of anti-Semitic literature. There is evidence that he provided financial backing to Adolf Hitler and received a medal from Mussolini as late as 1938. According to one source, Ford suffered a stroke in 1945 as he watched a newsreel of the liberation of the Nazi death camps. He died in 1947, at eighty-three.

At Age 46...

Sir Winston Churchill bombed Iraq.

As a promising young politician, Winston Leonard Spencer Churchill (Nov. 30, 1874–Jan. 24, 1965) was named First Lord of the Admiralty in 1911, a position he held in 1914 when World War I broke out. After promoting the assault on Gallipoli in 1915, which turned into a bloody fiasco, Churchill was forced out of government and went to the Western Front to command a battalion. Returning to the government, he became Colonial Secretary in 1921 and helped cobble together the new nation of Iraq out of fragments of the old Ottoman Empire. The Iraqis promptly rebelled against British rule. Rather than face the expense of a hundred-thousand-man occupation army, Churchill tried a more cost-effective means of subduing the Iraqis; he sent Royal Air Force squadrons to the region to bomb the Iraqis into submission. When that didn't work, he proposed even sterner measures: "I am strongly in favor of using poisoned gas against uncivilized tribes to spread a lively terror." Churchill's attempt to use Weapons of Mass Destruction in Iraq anticipated Saddam Hussein by more than half a century, but the proposal was rejected. Eventually, the British beat an inglorious retreat from Iraq, and Churchill again lost his place in government. By the 1930s, his career in eclipse, Churchill was a noisy but generally ignored Parliament back-bencher. History seemed to be finished with Winston Churchill.

At Age 47...

Vladimir Ilyich Lenin seized power in Russia.

The son of a Russian civil service worker named Ulyanov, Lenin (Apr. 22, 1870–Jan. 21, 1924) became radicalized in 1877 when his brother was hanged for complicity in the plot to assassinate Tsar Alexander III. Despite being expelled from school for his protest activities, Lenin managed to earn a law degree. Frequently arrested and exiled, he rose to the leadership of the Bolshevik faction among Russian radicals. Returning from Switzerland to St. Petersburg after the overthrow of the tsar in 1917, he led an uprising against the Provisional Government and was elected Chairman of the Council of People's Commissars. Lenin was both a high-minded theorist of revolutionary politics and a down-and-dirty practitioner of terror as a means of consolidating Communist power. He made peace with Germany, then led the fledgling Soviet Union through a bloody civil war. Although seriously wounded, he survived an assassination attempt in 1918 but began suffering a series of strokes in 1921; he retired in 1922 and died in 1924, at fifty-three. Although Lenin wanted no memorials, his body was embalmed and put on permanent display in Red Square.

At Age 48...

Theodore Roosevelt became the first American to win a Nobel Prize.

Born to a prominent and wealthy family in New York, Theodore Roosevelt (Oct. 27, 1858–Jan. 6, 1919) was a sickly youth, but in 1884, after his mother and first wife died on the same day, went to the Dakota Badlands to pursue a vigorous life as a rancher, big-game hunter, and sometime lawman. Returning to the East, he made a name as a writer and politician, serving as assistant secretary of the navy in the McKinley administration. In that post, he helped engineer the onset of the Spanish-American War in 1898, then resigned his job to become a lieutenant colonel of volunteers. He became a national hero for his role in the battle at San Juan Hill (actually, the charge was up Kettle Hill), and McKinley tapped him as running mate in 1900. When McKinley was assassinated, Roosevelt, at age forty-two, became the youngest American president ever (though not the youngest ever elected). He wielded presidential power with a "big stick," and promoted progressive policies, "trust-busting," conservation, and building the Panama Canal. In 1905, he brokered a peace settlement in the Russo-Japanese War. For that achievement, he received the Nobel Peace Prize in 1906, the first American so honored. Remembered as much for his personal style as for his political achievements, which were substantial, Teddy joined Washington, Jefferson, and Lincoln on Mount Rushmore as the greatest of American leaders.

At Age 49...

William Shakespeare's Globe Theater burned down after a special effects malfunction.

The greatest English writer, William Shakespeare (Apr. 23, 1564–Apr. 23, 1616) was born in the small town of Stratford, the son of an alderman and black-market wool merchant. He received a standard education for the time, but no higher learning. By the 1590s, he had made a reputation on the London stage and began writing plays, as well as performing in them. In 1603, Shakespeare's company constructed the famous Globe Theater, where most of his plays made their debut. On June 19, 1613, during a performance of Shakespeare's Henry VIII, sparks from the discharge of a cannon set the theater's thatched roof ablaze. It is said that `playgoers were so wrapped up in the performance that at first they didn't even notice that the theater was burning down around them.` In any case, there were no casualties except the theater itself, which burned to the ground. Evidently taking this as a good exit cue, Shakespeare retired to Stratford, where he continued to write until his death on his fifty-second birthday. Conspiracy theorists still maintain that Shakespeare was not really Shakespeare, or that someone else was—perhaps Francis Bacon, Christopher Marlowe, or Edward de Vere. That, of course, is a tale told by idiots, full of sound and fury, signifying nothing.

At Age 50...

Julius Caesar crossed
the Rubicon.

Born to a patrician Roman family, Gaius Julius Caesar (July 13, 100 BC–March 15, 44 BC) was an accomplished military leader whose campaigns in Gaul and Central Europe (58 BC–50 BC) were mainly the product of his personal ambition. As governor of Gaul, in 50 BC he was ordered to return to Rome and disband his army and was also forbidden to run for the Roman consulship. On January 10, 49 BC, Caesar made his fateful decision and crossed the Rubicon, a river in northern Italy, with his legions. "The die is cast," he declared. That act launched a civil war against his rival Pompey. By 48 BC, Caesar had defeated Pompey's numerically superior armies and had landed in Egypt, where Pompey was murdered. Caesar returned to Rome in 46 BC with Cleopatra and their infant son. The Senate declared him "dictator perpetuus" in 44 BC, but when Caesar began wearing purple—the color reserved for kings—his opponents decided the time had come to put an end to his seemingly unlimited ambitions. In the Senate on the Ides of March (March 15), Caesar was stabbed twenty-three times and fell, dead, in front of a statue of Pompey. The assassins said they were trying to save the Roman Republic, but in reality they plunged it into more than a decade of civil war, which ended only when Octavian became emperor in 27 BC. The Republic was as dead as Caesar.

At Age 51...

Leonardo da Vinci painted the *Mona Lisa*.

The quintessential Renaissance man, Leonardo (Apr. 15, 1452–May 2, 1519) was an illegitimate son who grew up in Florence and began painting in his early teens. Under the patronage of Cesare Borgia, Leonardo branched out from painting to sculpture, music, engineering, military architecture, and visionary inventions. His greatest works are considered to be *The Last Supper*, completed in 1498 in Milan, and the *Mona Lisa*, begun in 1503. Who was Mona Lisa? Historians have debated endlessly, proposing a number of possible candidates, most of them the wives of wealthy merchants or nobles. One theory even suggests that the painting is a self-portrait! The painting itself, done in oil on poplar wood, has had a storied history. It was stolen from the Paris Louvre in 1911 by an employee who simply walked out the door with the painting under his coat. It was recovered in 1913. In 1956, it was damaged when someone threw a beaker of acid at it. Today, it is on display in the Louvre behind bulletproof glass and is insured for a figure reported to be in excess of $600 million.

At Age 52...

Jimmy Carter was
elected president.

An obscure peanut farmer and one-term governor from Plains, Georgia, James Earl Carter Jr. (b. Oct. 1, 1924) was one of the more surprising choices for an American president. A graduate of the Naval Academy, Carter served for seven years as an engineer aboard nuclear submarines, then returned to Georgia and entered politics. He was elected governor in 1970. When he announced his candidacy for president in 1974, the general response was, "Jimmy who?" But in the wake of Vietnam and Watergate, voters were tired of career politicians and Washington insiders, and Carter's promise "I will never lie to you" struck a responsive chord. He defeated Gerald Ford in 1976, but his administration proved why insiders make more effective presidents than outsiders. Carter never seemed to master the give-and-take of Washington politics, and he didn't get much done, except in foreign affairs, where he brokered the Camp David accord between Israel and Egypt. An oil embargo and the Iranian hostage crisis doomed his presidency, and he lost to Ronald Reagan in 1980. But if he was a mediocre president, Carter turned out to be an outstanding ex-president. His work with Habitat for Humanity has been inspiring, and his role as an international advocate for human rights won him the Nobel Peace Prize in 2002.

At Age 53...

Dwight D. Eisenhower commanded the D-Day invasion of Normandy.

Raised in a humble family in Abilene, Kansas, Eisenhower (Oct. 14, 1890–Mar. 28, 1969) attended West Point in the Class of 1915 but missed combat in World War I and seemed destined to spend his career in a series of dreary staff jobs. He was an assistant to Douglas MacArthur, who called Ike "the best file clerk in the army." In turn, Eisenhower said he "studied dramatics" under MacArthur. But Chief of Staff George Marshall had noticed Eisenhower's abilities and called him to Washington after Pearl Harbor to help plan the war effort. Eisenhower rose swiftly from colonel to general and was given command of the first American offensive against Germany, the invasion of North Africa in November 1942. Promoted to four-star rank and named overall Allied commander in Europe, `Eisenhower gave the fateful "go" decision on June 5, 1944, launching the mammoth D-Day invasion of France.` According to some historians, June 6, 1944, was the most important day of the twentieth century, for it assured that Western Europe would be dominated by neither the Nazis nor the advancing Soviets under Stalin. Riding herd on flamboyant and egotistical Allied generals like Montgomery and Patton, Eisenhower led his armies to victory over Germany in May 1945. Everyone liked Ike, and in 1952 he was elected president, serving two terms.

At Age 54...

Queen Liliuokalani was overthrown.

The last queen to rule over what was to become American soil, Lydia Paki Kamekeha Liliuokalani (Sept. 2, 1838–Nov. 11, 1917) became queen of the Hawaiian Islands on January 17, 1891, following the death of her brother, Kalakaua. At the time, American fruit and sugar growers held most of the power in the Islands and were maneuvering to seize them for the United States. Liliuokalani resisted these maneuvers, so early in 1893 American minister John L. Stevens ordered troops from the USS *Boston* to go ashore and "protect" the Iolani Palace and other government buildings. The coup deposed Liliuokalani, and the Republic of Hawaii was proclaimed, with pineapple baron Sanford B. Dole as its president. Liliuokalani initially had the sympathy of U.S. president Grover Cleveland, who offered to restore her crown if she agreed to pardon the plotters. Liliuokalani refused the deal and was briefly imprisoned. While in confinement, the musically inclined queen composed the enduring Hawaiian classic "Aloha Oe." Hawaii was formally annexed by the United States in 1898 and became the fiftieth state in 1959—the only American state once ruled by a queen.

At Age 55...

Rachel Carson published *Silent Spring*.

Beginning her career as a biologist with the U.S. Bureau of Fisheries, Rachel Carson (May 27, 1907–Apr. 14, 1964) is known today as the mother of the modern environmental movement. Resigning from her government job in 1952 to devote herself to writing, she began *Silent Spring* in 1957 and published it in 1962. The book details the harmful effects of pesticides, especially DDT, and made many Americans aware, for the first time, that the natural world they had taken for granted was imperiled by pollution. One of the principal victims of DDT was the national symbol—the bald eagle, whose eggshells became dangerously fragile when exposed to the chemical. DDT was also showing up in mother's milk as the toxin made its way through the food chain. President John F. Kennedy read her book and was motivated to order federal testing for the chemicals Carson had mentioned. Eight years later, after "green" politics had become popular, President Nixon announced the creation of the Environmental Protection Agency. In the years since then, DDT contamination has declined, and the bald eagle has made a comeback.

At Age 56...

George Washington
was elected president—
unanimously.

If ever there was an indispensable man, it was George Washington (Feb. 22, 1732–Dec. 14, 1799). Probably the wealthiest man in the American colonies, Washington had served with the British Army during the French and Indian War and showed up at the Continental Congress in Philadelphia in 1775 wearing a military uniform. Congress needed to select an overall commander for the colonial troops then besieging the British in Boston. Boston merchant and smuggler John Hancock, the presiding officer of the congress, wanted the job for himself. But John Adams realized that it was imperative to win the support of the middle and southern colonies for the cause and successfully maneuvered to get the position for Washington, a Virginian. As a general, Washington was cautious and methodical, always aware that the continued survival of his army was the *sine qua non* for American success. When the Constitution was adopted in 1789, there was only one possible choice for first president. Washington was elected unanimously by the electoral college. He served two terms and may have performed his most important service to the nation by voluntarily retiring in 1797; America would have no "president-for-life." He fell ill in 1799 and probably was killed inadvertently by his doctors, who subscribed to the ancient practice of bleeding a patient. Washington is buried at his beloved Mt. Vernon.

At Age 57...

Geronimo finally surrendered to the army.

Born on Apache land in what was then Mexico (now New Mexico), Geronimo (June 16, 1829–Feb. 17, 1909) became one of the most famous of all Native Americans who opposed white encroachment on their territory. Growing up as a medicine man among the Chiricahua Apaches, his name was Goyathlay ("One Who Yawns"), but the Mexicans called him "Jerome," or "Geronimo." In 1848, the Mexicans slaughtered most of his family, and he spent the next four decades making them regret it. When the Americans displaced the Mexicans in the Southwest, Geronimo fought them as well. He was captured and escaped several times—unlike many Indian leaders, such as Crazy Horse, who were "killed while trying to escape." Geronimo led a hit-and-run war against the American army, vanishing with his people into the mountains and deserts. His was the last organized resistance against the army among Native American peoples, but finally, on September 4, 1886, he surrendered to General Nelson Miles, at Skeleton Canyon, Arizona. He lived out his final years at Fort Sill, Oklahoma, and was never allowed to return to his native lands. Nevertheless, he became something of a celebrity; he sold his photograph to tourists and appeared in Theodore Roosevelt's inaugural parade in 1905.

At Age 58...

Charlemagne was crowned Holy Roman Emperor.

The elder son of Pepin the Short, Charles the Great, or Charlemagne (742–Jan. 28, 814) was a Frankish king and ferocious warrior who brought Europe the most unity it had seen since the fall of the Roman Empire. He learned to read only as an adult and probably never learned to write; yet he presided over what is known as the Carolingian Renaissance, a flowering of scholarship and art during his era. After many battles, he conquered Saxony and converted its population to Christianity—on pain of execution. He tried but failed to conquer Spain. In Rome on Christmas Day, 800, Pope Leo III crowned Charlemagne emperor, reviving the title for the first time in over three hundred years. Charlemagne organized his empire into some three hundred fifty counties or districts, each of them accountable to the emperor. The empire brought the first glimmerings of cultural and political unity to Western Europe but, as was later observed, it wasn't really holy, Roman, or an empire.

At Age 59...

Clara Barton founded the American Red Cross.

Although she had no medical training, Clarissa Harlowe Barton (Dec. 25, 1821–Apr. 12, 1912) became the most famous nurse in American history. After working as a teacher for many years, she took a job in the Washington Patent Office just before the Civil War. When the Union defeat at Bull Run in June 1861 produced thousands of casualties, Barton organized an effort to procure the necessary medical supplies. She followed the Union armies in Virginia, providing what medical help she could. In 1864, General Benjamin Butler named her superintendent of nurses in his department. President Lincoln put her in charge of a systematic effort to account for more than thirty thousand Union troops who were missing in action, and she also reported on conditions at the infamous Confederate prison at Andersonville, Georgia. In 1881, Barton became one of the founders and the first president of the American Red Cross. The Johnstown Flood in Pennsylvania in 1889, in which more than twenty-two hundred people died, was the first large-scale relief effort mounted by Barton and her organization. She resigned as president in 1904, at eighty-two.

At Age 60...

Richard Nixon told the world, "I'm not a crook!"

The only president ever to resign from office, Richard Milhous Nixon (Jan. 9, 1913–Apr. 22, 1994) was elected to Congress in 1946 and immediately established a reputation as an energetic young Red-baiter during the McCarthy era. Eisenhower tapped him as running mate in 1952 but never particularly cared for him. After a narrow loss to Kennedy in 1960, Nixon won the presidency in 1968. A paranoid, solitary man who kept a list of his many enemies, Nixon won a landslide reelection in 1972, but during the campaign a group of secret operatives directed from the White House were arrested during a break-in at the Democratic headquarters in the Watergate hotel. As the investigation of the incident developed, evidence emerged that the Watergate burglary was only one of a coordinated series of clandestine operations run by people close to Nixon. Known as "Tricky Dicky" twenty years before Watergate, Nixon stonewalled it and continued to deny his involvement in the affair. At a press conference on November 17, 1973, he famously declared, "I'm not a crook!" But the evidence indicated otherwise, and Nixon resigned on August 8, 1974, rather than face impeachment. In his later years, Nixon tried to rehabilitate his image as a statesman, but without much success.

At Age 61...

Benito Mussolini was
executed by partisans…
or perhaps someone else.

The son of a blacksmith who was named for Mexican revolutionary Benito Juarez, Mussolini (July 29, 1883–Apr. 28, 1945) abandoned his early socialist beliefs and became the first practitioner of fascism, which relied on state-sponsored terror, propaganda, and a cult of personality surrounding "Il Duce." He was head of the Italian state from 1922 until 1943 and "made the trains run on time." His attempts to establish a neo-Roman Empire in Africa and the Mediterranean would have been laughable if they hadn't been so tragic. When Allied troops landed in Sicily in 1943, Mussolini was stripped of his powers by King Victor Emmanuel and placed under arrest. A daring raid by Nazi commandos freed him, and Hitler installed him as a puppet ruler in northern Italy. With Allied troops closing in, Mussolini was captured by Italian partisans when he attempted to flee to Switzerland. He was shot on April 28, 1945—just two days before Hitler would commit suicide—and his body was hung from a lamppost in the street. Recent evidence has emerged suggesting that Mussolini actually may have been killed by British agents, who supposedly wanted to suppress the release of a secret correspondence between Mussolini and Churchill. However, this conspiracy theory remains unsubstantiated.

At Age 62...

Alfred Nobel
established the
Nobel Peace Prize.

Born in Sweden, Alfred Bernhard Nobel (Oct. 21, 1833–Dec. 10, 1896) was a chemist who set up a nitroglycerin factory in Hamburg, Germany, in 1865. The following year, the factory was destroyed in an explosion. Searching for a way to make nitro safer, Nobel worked on a raft anchored in the Elbe. He discovered that adding the substance kieselguhr to nitro produced a safe, doughy substance, which he called dynamite and patented it in 1867. He soon became fabulously wealthy and devoted his attention to the very profitable development of munitions. Still, like advocates of the machine gun, poison gas, and nuclear weapons, Nobel believed that his inventions might end, or at least deter, war. He told a peace advocate, `Perhaps my factories will put an end to war sooner than your congresses`; on the day that two army corps can mutually annihilate each other in a second, all civilized nations will surely recoil in horror and disband their troops." Unfortunately, that never happened. In a will written in 1895 Nobel devoted a portion of his fortune to the establishment of a prize to be awarded annually to the person who had done the most to promote peace. The first winners, in 1901, were Henry Dunant, founder of the International Red Cross, and pacifist Frederic Passy. Other winners include: Theodore Roosevelt, Woodrow Wilson, Jane Addams, Ralph Bunche, Albert Schweitzer, George C. Marshall, Martin Luther King Jr., Henry Kissinger, Andrei Sakharov, Amnesty International, Menachem Begin, Anwar Sadat, Mother Teresa, Lech Walesa, Desmond Tutu, Mikhail Gorbachev, Nelson Mandela, Yitzhak Rabin, Yasser Arafat, and Jimmy Carter.

At Age 63...

Nikita Khrushchev led
the world into the
Space Age.

The grandson of a serf, the son of an illiterate coal miner, and a pipefitter by trade, Nikita Sergeyevich Khrushchev (Apr. 5, 1894–Sept. 11, 1971) entered politics following the Bolshevik Revolution in 1917. Rising through the Communist Party ranks, he served as a general at Stalingrad and became First Secretary of the Party in 1953, following Stalin's death. He skillfully maneuvered to remove his competition and was the undisputed ruler of the USSR by 1958. In 1956, he began a campaign of "de-Stalinization," designed to correct some of the worst abuses of the Communist system. But Khrushchev was mainly concerned with meeting the Cold War challenge of the West. On October 4, 1957, the Soviet Union launched the first artificial Earth-orbiting satellite, *Sputnik I*. That very well may have been the high-water mark of the Soviet Union's seven-decade history, for it deeply alarmed the West and convinced many in the Third World that the Communist system was capable of great achievements. Yet *Sputnik* was really a latter-day "Potemkin village"—all front and no back. Despite fears of a "missile gap," the Soviets lagged behind the West in rocket technology and economic strength. After the Cuban Missile Crisis of 1962 exposed Khrushchev's dangerous bluster, he was removed from power in 1964. But under his leadership, mankind had broken the bonds of Earth and made its first foray into outer space.

At Age 64...

Douglas MacArthur returned to the Philippines.

The son of a Civil War hero, Douglas MacArthur (Jan. 26, 1880–Apr. 5, 1964) grew up on a series of army posts in the American West and attended West Point. Serving with conspicuous gallantry in World War I, MacArthur was promoted to brigadier general, the youngest ever to achieve that rank in the regular (as opposed to volunteer) army. With an outsized ego and an imperial manner, MacArthur rose to command the peacetime army but sullied his reputation by ordering a violent assault on the peaceful "Bonus Army"—a band of World War I veterans who were trying to get promised bonus payments in the depths of the Depression. As commander of American and Philippine forces, he was caught unprepared by the Japanese attack on December 8, 1941, despite the bombing of Pearl Harbor in Hawaii the previous day. MacArthur presided over a stunning American defeat by the Japanese in the Philippines and was ordered to escape to Australia in a PT boat. Upon arrival there, he declared "I shall return." The War Department tried to get him to change that to, "We shall return," but MacArthur refused. And he did return. After leading a brilliant campaign in New Guinea, MacArthur waded ashore on the Philippine island of Leyte on October 20, 1944. Less than a year later, on September 2, 1945, he accepted the Japanese surrender on the battleship Missouri in Tokyo Bay.

At Age 65...

"Old Rough and Ready" was done in by cherries and milk.

One of a long line of American generals who became president, Zachary Taylor (Nov. 24, 1784–July 9, 1850) won the affectionate nickname of "Old Rough and Ready" from his troops during his successful campaign in northern Mexico. The Whigs, whose only previous president had also been a general—William Henry Harrison, who died in 1841 after a month in office—nominated Taylor to run in 1848. Taylor proved to be a forceful president. Although he was a southerner and a slaveholder, he was a committed nationalist and threatened to hang anyone who tried to secede from the Union, starting with his former son-in-law, Jefferson Davis. (Nevertheless, Taylor's son, Richard, later became a Confederate general.) Taylor opposed the Compromise of 1850, which would have extended slavery into formerly free territories. But at a Fourth of July celebration in 1850, Taylor overindulged in cherries and milk and soon fell ill with an intestinal disorder. He died a few days later and was succeeded by Millard Fillmore, who approved the Compromise. It had long been rumored that Taylor was poisoned by slavery proponents, but his body was recently disinterred and no trace of poison was found.

At Age 66...

Tamerlane won his last
great victory.

Born near Samarkand in modern Uzbekistan, Tamerlane (1336–Feb. 1405)—or Timur Lenk, meaning "Timur the Lame," due to partial paralysis on his left side—began his military career about 1358 and became sovereign in 1369. Over the next thirty years, he led a campaign of conquest and expansion from the Volga and the Urals to Persia and India. Said to be a descendant of Genghis Khan, Tamerlane was not interested in empire, just looting. The Indian city of Delhi took over a century to rebuild after Tamerlane's troops plundered it. After one battle, he executed one hundred thousand Indian soldiers and once slaughtered twenty thousand residents of Damascus. He left huge pyramids of human skulls to mark the sites of his victories. In 1402 he invaded Anatolia and won his last great victory, over the Ottomans at Ankara. He began an invasion of China late in 1404 but came down with a fever and died early in 1405 at the age of about sixty-eight. He is remembered as the last of the great nomad warriors.

At Age 67...

Edgar Rice Burroughs
became the oldest
war correspondent in
World War II.

The son of a Civil War veteran, Burroughs (Sept. 1, 1875–Mar. 19, 1950) enlisted in the Seventh Cavalry after failing to gain admission to West Point. He "chased but never caught" Apaches in the Southwest, then left the army due to a heart ailment. He tried his hand at a variety of odd jobs and business ventures with little success. In 1911, while working as a pencil-sharpener wholesaler, he decided to turn to writing for the cheap pulp magazines he enjoyed reading. "If people were paid to write rot such as I read," he said, "I could write stories just as rotten." He sold his first story, "Under the Moons of Mars," and made four hundred dollars on it. In 1912, he wrote the first of his Tarzan stories. Enjoying phenomenally popular success with his tales of jungle men, Martian princesses, and lost worlds, he bought a ranch north of Los Angeles and named it Tarzana. When the area was later incorporated, the residents kept the name, making Tarzana, California, the only city ever named after a fictional character. Living in Hawaii at the time of the Japanese attack on Pearl Harbor, Burroughs signed up as a war correspondent, the oldest of the war. He covered campaigns in the Pacific and even flew on bombing missions with the Seventh Air Force. He died at seventy-four, one of the most successful authors of the twentieth century.

At Age 68...

William Henry Harrison
talked himself to death.

In the presidential election of 1840, the Whig party decided to run a general of their own to counter the lingering aura of Andrew Jackson. They found their man in William Henry Harrison (Feb. 9, 1773–Apr. 4, 1841), a famous Indian fighter who had served as an aide to Mad Anthony Wayne in the Battle of Fallen Timbers in 1794. He served as governor of Indiana Territory from 1801 to 1813 and commanded the troops that defeated the great Indian warrior Tecumseh at the Battle of Tippecanoe, in 1811. His 1840 presidential campaign was recognizably modern in some respects, complete with a memorable slogan—"Tippecanoe and Tyler, too!" The Whigs won the election and Harrison was inaugurated on a cold, rainy day in March 1841. Unfortunately, he chose to deliver a long—nine thousand words—oration that lasted nearly two hours. Harrison caught a cold that soon developed into pneumonia and died on April 4, after less than a month in office. At 68, he was the oldest president elected until Ronald Reagan in 1980. His grandson, Benjamin, was elected president in 1888. Admirers of William Henry Harrison make a case that he was the greatest president in U.S. history, because he arguably did less harm to the Republic than any other president.

At Age 69...

Galileo Galilei was convicted of heresy and sentenced to life imprisonment.

Galileo (Feb. 15, 1564–Jan. 8, 1642) was born in Pisa, and he became a professor at the University of Padua in 1589. One of the greatest thinkers of any era, he helped introduce scientific method and experimental science. He built his first telescope in 1609, and by 1610 had discovered the moons of Jupiter and the phases of Venus. His observations led him to adopt the Copernican heliocentric viewpoint, which he announced publicly in 1616. The notion that the sun was the center of the solar system conflicted with officially approved cosmology; the Catholic Church declared that his view was false and ordered him not to espouse it. But in 1632, Galileo published a book in which, in dialogue form, he presented a defense of heliocentrism. Put on trial in 1633, at the age of sixty-nine, Galileo was convicted of heresy. He was sentenced to spend the rest of his life under house arrest, and the Inquisition put his works on the *Index of Prohibited Books*. In 1992, three hundred fifty years after his death, the Church admitted that errors had been made in Galileo's case, although it did not admit that it had been wrong in convicting him of heresy.

At Age 70...

Golda Meir became
Prime Minister of
Israel.

Born Goldie Mabovitch in Kiev (May 3, 1898–Dec. 8, 1978), young Golda's first memory was of an anti-Jewish pogrom. She and her family emigrated to Milwaukee in 1906, but the strong-minded girl ran away to Denver at the age of fourteen rather than marry an older man selected by her family. There, in 1917, she married a sign painter named Morris Myerson. Golda graduated from college and became a teacher and a committed Zionist. She and her husband emigrated to the British Mandate of Palestine in 1921, where she lived for a time on a kibbutz and became active in politics. In 1948, she was one of twenty-four signers of the Declaration of the Establishment of the State of Israel. From 1949 to 1956 she served as Israeli labor minister. Prime Minister David Ben-Gurion called her "the only man in the Cabinet." At Ben-Gurion's request, she changed her name to a Hebrew name, selecting Meir, which means "to burn brightly." Called out of retirement following the death of Prime Minister Levi Eshkol, she became prime minister on March 17, 1969, at the age of seventy. She was only the third woman in world history to reach such a position. She resigned on April 11, 1974, following controversy over her leadership during the Yom Kippur War of October 1973. A tough and determined leader, she once said, "You cannot shake hands with a clenched fist."

At Age 71...

Douglas MacArthur
was fired by
Harry Truman.

After the Allied victory in World War II, Douglas MacArthur (Jan. 26, 1880–Apr. 5, 1964) commanded the occupation forces in Japan and helped rebuild the country as a modern democratic state. When North Korean armies crossed the thirty-eighth parallel and invaded South Korea in June 1950, American forces were ill-prepared to oppose them. As United Nations troops held onto the Pusan perimeter, MacArthur launched a risky but successful amphibious landing at Inchon, behind North Korean lines. The UN forces soon crossed the thirty-eighth parallel in pursuit of the shattered Communist armies. MacArthur flew to Wake Island for a meeting with President Harry Truman in October, claiming he was too busy to go to Washington. Treating the former artillery captain with barely concealed contempt, MacArthur assured the president that the war would be over by Christmas. But by then, hundreds of thousands of Chinese "volunteers" had administered a crushing defeat to MacArthur's surprised command. MacArthur issued public calls for the use of nuclear weapons against China. `Truman had no intention of letting the Korean conflict become World War III` and ordered MacArthur to be quiet. MacArthur didn't, so in April 1951 Truman fired him for insubordination. MacArthur had hopes of being elected president in 1952, but the voters—many of them former GIs who had never liked "Dugout Doug"—preferred another general, Eisenhower. MacArthur "just faded away" and died in 1964.

At Age 72...

Mao Zedong launched
the Cultural Revolution.

One of the great figures of the twentieth century, Mao Zedong (Dec. 26, 1893–Sept. 9, 1976) had been leader of the Chinese Communist Party ever since the epic Long March of 1935. After defeating the Nationalist forces of Chiang Kai-shek in 1949, he set about turning China into a modern industrial state. His "Great Leap Forward," relying on backyard blast furnaces, didn't accomplish much, and by the sixties Mao was more or less on the sidelines of Chinese leadership. Attempting to reestablish his authority and purge the Party of what he considered to be impurities, he enlisted the young Red Guards, who launched a campaign of terror and intimidation against Mao's rivals. Thousands of intellectuals were sent to concentration camps in the country to be "reeducated." Thousands more—perhaps hundreds of thousands—were executed. By 1969, Mao was once again firmly in charge of China. But within a month of his death in 1976, the radicals—including Mao's wife and the infamous "Gang of Four"—were arrested as Communist China sought accommodation with the West and Deng Xiaoping began his rise to power.

At Age 73...

Ronald Reagan became the oldest man to win a presidential election.

A smiling, affable Midwesterner, Ronald Wilson Reagan (Feb. 6, 1911–June 5, 2004) started out as a sportscaster, then took a Hollywood screen test in 1937 and went on to make fifty-three movies. He first became involved in politics as president of the Screen Actors Guild, then was elected governor of California in 1966. After two unsuccessful attempts, he won the Republican presidential nomination in 1980 and defeated Jimmy Carter in a landslide. He survived an assassination attempt in early 1981, an event that gave him a large fund of popular goodwill; after the assassinations and failed presidencies of the sixties and seventies, Americans were eager to see a president survive and succeed. He ran for reelection in 1984, at the age of seventy-three. When his opponent, Walter Mondale, attempted to raise the issue of age, Reagan laughed it off by promising not to make an issue of his challenger's youth. Reagan had promised to submit to regular examinations for senility but never did. After he left office, it was revealed that he suffered from Alzheimer's disease, raising uncomfortable questions about just when the symptoms first appeared. After a long, twilight struggle against the ailment, he died in 2004, at the age of ninety-three.

At Age 74...

Katharine Hepburn
won her fourth Oscar.

The feisty, independent daughter of a feisty, independent Connecticut family, Katharine Hepburn (May 12, 1907–June 29, 2003) graduated from Bryn Mawr in 1928 and began her acting career in New York the same year. An early marriage failed, and she divorced in 1934, never to remarry. By then, she had moved to Hollywood, where she won her first Best Actress Oscar, for Morning Glory in 1934. Assertive and outspoken, Hepburn challenged the power of the Hollywood studio barons, earning her their enmity and the label "Box Office Poison." At the suggestion of her lover at the time, Howard Hughes, she bought the movie rights to her hit play The Philadelphia Story and used it to revitalize her film career. About this time, she met and fell in love with Spencer Tracy. A married and devout Catholic, Tracy never divorced but maintained a close relationship with Hepburn—on and off the screen—for the rest of his life. Hepburn won her second Oscar for her last film with Tracy, Guess Who's Coming to Dinner in 1968. The following year, she won a record third Oscar for her performance as Eleanor of Aquitaine in The Lion in Winter. Hepburn's final Oscar came in 1982 for On Golden Pond, in which she played opposite Henry Fonda. Her total of twelve Best Actress nominations were a record until 2003, when Meryl Streep received a thirteenth nomination. A true American original, Katharine Hepburn was the stuff of legends. She died in 2003 at the age of ninety-six.

At Age 75...

Henry Fonda appeared in a role that won him his first and only Oscar.

It is surprising to realize that Henry Fonda (May 16, 1905–Aug. 12, 1982), the veteran of over a hundred movies and the founder of a Hollywood dynasty now in its third generation, never won an Academy Award as Best Actor until his final theatrical film. Beginning his career on the New York stage in 1926, he went to Hollywood in 1935 and appeared in some of the classic films of his era. And yet, he never won an Oscar—and received only one nomination—until his final film role in *On Golden Pond*, which was released in 1981, when Fonda was seventy-five. Playing crotchety old Norman Thayer opposite Katharine Hepburn and his real-life daughter, Jane, Fonda finally received the golden statue in 1982, just a few months before his death. His only other nomination came in 1941 for *The Grapes of Wrath*, but he lost to James Stewart for *The Philadelphia Story*, in which, ironically, Stewart played opposite Katharine Hepburn. Somehow the Academy never recognized Fonda for his work in such classics as *Mr. Roberts*, *Twelve Angry Men*, and *Fail-Safe*. That probably says more about Hollywood than it does about Fonda, one of the greatest actors in film history.

At Age 76...

Sir Winston Churchill
became prime minister
for the second time.

In the late 1930s, Winston Leonard Spencer Churchill (Nov. 30, 1874–Jan. 24, 1965) was a middle-aged has-been, his career seemingly in total eclipse. But when war broke out in 1939, he was appointed First Lord of the Admiralty, a role he had filled in World War I. As German armies poured into France and the Low Countries in May 1940, Neville Chamberlain's government collapsed, and Churchill, at the age of sixty-five, was named prime minister. Ironically, the dark days that followed were Britain's—and Churchill's—finest hour. Britain fought on alone against the Nazis for over a year, until the Soviet Union and the United States entered the war. Churchill chafed in the role of junior partner to Roosevelt in the Grand Alliance but soldiered on with bulldog determination. Shortly after the defeat of Germany, British voters swept Churchill and the Conservatives from office. After six years as leader of the opposition, Churchill returned to office in 1951 with the defeat of the Atlee government in a general election. Now seventy-six, his powers diminishing, Churchill's second term as prime minister was not a success, as he grappled ineffectively with a series of domestic problems and foreign crises. He resigned in 1955, at the age of eighty, and died a decade later, his place in history secure.

At Age 77...

John Glenn
became the oldest man
to fly in space.

A genuine American legend, John Herschel Glenn (b. July 18, 1921) was a Marine pilot who flew fifty-nine combat missions in World War II and twenty-seven more in Korea (where his wingman was Hall of Fame ballplayer Ted Williams). Joining NASA's Astronaut Corps as one of the Original Seven in 1959, Glenn became the first American to orbit the Earth with his flight of February 20, 1962. He retired from NASA, entered politics, and was elected to the U.S. Senate from Ohio in 1974. His public image as "Mr. Clean Marine" was reinforced by Tom Wolfe's book *The Right Stuff* and the subsequent movie, although it didn't help him in his presidential campaign of 1984. But Glenn did campaign successfully to win another trip to orbit. Using his name, legend, and political pull, in 1998, at the age of seventy-seven, Glenn won a slot in the crew of the space shuttle *Discovery*. Ostensibly, his role was as a subject for medical research on aging, which in some ways resembled the effects of exposure to zero-gravity. The flight—Oct. 29–Nov. 7, 1998—was successful, and John Glenn, the oldest man ever to fly in space, returned to Earth—thirty-six years after his first flight—with no ill effects.

At Age 78...

William Randolph Hearst saw a movie he didn't like—*Citizen Kane.*

The son of a millionaire mining magnate and U.S. senator, William Randolph Hearst (Apr. 29, 1863–Aug. 14, 1951) entered the world of publishing at the age of twenty-three in 1887, when his father took over the San Francisco Examiner in payment for a gambling debt. Moving on to the New York Journal in 1895, Hearst became the successful and powerful purveyor of "yellow journalism." He built a national newspaper empire and did more than anyone else to invent the Spanish-American War. He served briefly in Congress but failed in his attempt to be elected governor of New York. In 1903, he married a chorus girl twenty years his junior, a marriage that lasted until 1926. He spent his later years in the company of his mistress, actress Marion Davies, at his two-hundred-forty-thousand-acre "castle" in San Simeon, California. If all of this sounds vaguely familiar, you've probably seen Citizen Kane. The 1941 movie created by "Boy Wonder" Orson Welles was a thinly disguised satire on Hearst's life, and Hearst wasn't happy about it. He denounced the film in his papers and at one point attempted to buy all the copies and negatives of Kane and have them burned. His campaign probably accounted for the film's box office flop, which hurt Welles's career, but Welles had the last laugh. Citizen Kane is widely regarded as the greatest movie ever made, and to the extent that Hearst is remembered at all today, it is mostly because of Kane.

At Age 79...

Grandma Moses had her first art exhibition.

A farmer's wife and mother of five, Anna Mary Robertson (Sept. 7, 1860–Dec. 13, 1961) didn't take up painting until she was in her mid-seventies. Her first effort was in the medium of house paint. An art collector happened to notice some of her work in a drugstore window and in 1939 arranged for an exhibition at a gallery in New York. Robertson attracted attention, and soon her art was winning awards and being exhibited in museums. Known as a primitive artist, she was self-taught and painted scenes of American rural life in a colorful, naturalistic style. Her subjects were oaken buckets, Thanksgiving turkeys, and family reunions. "I like to paint old-timey things," she told Edward R. Murrow in a 1955 television interview. She did the illustrations for a book of *The Night Before Christmas* at the age of one hundred and produced twenty-five paintings in the final year of her life. She died in 1961 at the age of 101.

At Age 80...

Aaron Burr
was divorced.

A veteran of the Revolutionary War, Aaron Burr (Feb. 6, 1756–Sept. 14, 1836) ran for president on the same ticket as Thomas Jefferson in 1800. Under the system at the time, the second-place finisher became vice president. But Jefferson and Burr got seventy-three electoral votes apiece, and Burr refused to concede the top spot. Opposition Federalists preferred Burr and maneuvered to get him elected president. However, Federalist Alexander Hamilton wouldn't support the plan, and Burr eventually lost. He served as vice president, but Jefferson had no use for him; he was not included on the ticket in 1804. That year, his long-running feud with Hamilton culminated in a duel, in which Burr shot and killed Hamilton. He was indicted for murder but never tried. Out of office, Burr became embroiled in a shadowy plot to create an independent nation west of the Appalachians. The plot was betrayed and Burr was tried for treason; he was acquitted due to the absence of key witnesses against him. After several years in exile, Burr settled into life as a New York attorney. He married a wealthy widow, Elizabeth Bowen Jumel, in 1833, but they soon separated when Elizabeth discovered that Burr was wasting her fortune in speculation. She sued for a divorce, which was granted on September 14, 1836—the day Burr died.

At Age 81...

George Burns
played God.

The cigar-smoking, wise-cracking George Burns (Jan. 20, 1896–Mar. 9, 1996) was a comedy legend who got his start in Vaudeville early in the twentieth century. He made his first movie in 1929 and his last in 1994, at the age of ninety-eight. He was best known for his long-running act with his second wife, Gracie Allen, who retired in 1958 and died in 1964. The ditsy Allen and wise-guy Burns starred in a radio series from 1932 to 1950 and then moved on to television from 1950 to 1958. In 1977, at eighty-one, Burns got the role of God in the comedy film *Oh, God!* The film was a huge hit, won Burns a new generation of fans, and spawned two sequels. He continued performing on Broadway and in Las Vegas and promised to play Vegas on his hundredth birthday. But by then, age had finally caught up with Burns, and he was unable to make the date. He died six weeks later.

At Age 82...

Marshal Tito
was named
President for Life.

Born Josip Broz in what was then Austria-Hungary, Tito (May 7, 1892–May 4, 1980) fought in World War I and was captured by the Russians. While in Russia, he joined the Communist Party and fought for the Red Guard during the Russian Civil War. Returning home to the newly created nation of Yugoslavia, he continued his Communist activities, and by the thirties had taken the Party name of Tito. When the Germans occupied Yugoslavia in 1941, Tito led the resistance movement. He consolidated his power after the war and became the Yugoslav leader. Although he was a Communist, he refused to knuckle under to the demands of Soviet leader Joseph Stalin. He was expelled from the Cominform in 1948 and followed a policy of nonalignment during the Cold War. He became the leader of a large bloc of neutral nations, playing off East against West but subservient to neither. On May 16, 1974, when Tito was eighty-two, the Yugoslav Assembly named him President for Life. He remained active, making international tours as late as 1979. He died in 1980 at the age of eighty-seven; within a decade, Yugoslavia itself had broken up.

At Age 83...

Thomas Edison received his 1,093rd—and last—patent.

Known as the "Wizard of Menlo Park," Thomas Alva Edison (Feb. 11, 1847–Oct. 18, 1931) is the most prolific inventor in American history, holding a record 1,093 patents. Building on his experience as a telegraph operator, Edison began tinkering with other electrical devices and came up with the first stock-ticker and various improvements to telegraphy. His first great success was the phonograph, in 1877. He is credited with inventing the electric light bulb, but—like most of his inventions—it was actually the result of a team effort in his laboratory. With no higher education, Edison was ignorant of many aspects of mathematics and science and favored a brute-force method of investigation. One employee, Nikola Tesla, said that if Edison were required to find a needle in a haystack, he would have methodically examined every last straw in the stack. "I was a sorry witness of such doings," said Tesla, "knowing that a little theory and calculation would have saved him 90 percent of his labor." For his part, Edison simply said, `Genius is 1 percent inspiration, 99 percent perspiration.` It also seemed to involve a lot of litigation, as Edison was frequently in court defending the originality of his inventions. He applied for his final patent, #1908280, "a holder for articles to be electroplated," in 1931, at the age of eighty-three.

At Age 84...

Phillipe Pétain became the leader of Vichy France.

The French general who led the defense of Verdun in 1915, Henri-Philippe Pétain (Apr. 24, 1856–July 23, 1951) recognized that the power of modern weapons gave a decisive advantage to defense over offense. Accordingly, he opposed the disastrous and bloody offensives favored by other French generals. In 1917, he achieved overall command of French forces, although it was Ferdinand Foch who received credit for the successful offensive of 1918. Pétain retired in 1934 but was called to duty again in 1940, after the German invasion had resulted in the occupation of much of the country. France capitulated, and Pétain was named to lead the collaborationist regime based at Vichy. When the Allies landed in Normandy in 1944, Pétain was spirited away to Germany but returned to France in 1945 and was charged with treason. He was tried, convicted, and sentenced to death; but in view of his age and previous service to France, the sentence was commuted to life in prison. Pétain died in prison in 1951 at the age of ninety-five.

At Age 85...

Bertrand Russell tried
to ban the bomb.

One of the great minds of the twentieth century, Bertrand Arthur William Russell (May 18, 1872–Feb. 2, 1970) was born to an aristocratic family in Victorian England (his grandfather had been prime minister) and began his studies at Cambridge University, where he became a professor at Trinity College in 1908. His work in mathematics, language, and philosophy earned him a Nobel Prize for Literature in 1950. His *Principia Mathematica* has been hailed as one of the great works of the century, and his contributions to the analysis of language, logic, and philosophy are regarded as seminal. Russell was also a lifelong pacifist and was jailed for six months for his opposition to British participation in World War I. He modified his views with the rise of Hitler and admitted that while war was always evil, in some circumstances it might be regarded as the lesser of multiple evils. Following the war, he was alarmed by the growth of nuclear stockpiles and teamed with Albert Einstein to issue an anti-nuclear manifesto. In 1957, at the age of eighty-five, he was a prime mover in organizing the Pugwash Conferences on Science and World Affairs and became the founding president of the Campaign for Nuclear Disarmament in 1958. As late as 1961, he was imprisoned for a week for leading Ban the Bomb demonstrations. He died in 1970, at the age of ninety-seven.

At Age 86...

Oliver Wendell Holmes Jr.
got Al Capone.

The son of the famed essayist and poet, Oliver Wendell Holmes Jr. (Mar. 8, 1841–Mar. 6, 1935) served in some of the greatest battles of the Civil War, then turned to a career in law. He was appointed to the Supreme Court by Theodore Roosevelt in 1902 and served until his resignation in 1932. In May 1927, Holmes—then age eighty-six—delivered the Court's opinion in the Sullivan case, which concerned a Prohibition bootlegger who had been charged with income tax evasion. A lower court had held that while illegal income may have been taxable, the self-incrimination protections of the Fifth Amendment meant that Sullivan was not required to file a tax return. The Supreme Court overturned the lower court decision, with Holmes declaring, "We are of the opinion that the protection of the Fifth Amendment was stretched too far." On the basis of this decision, the government was able to prosecute and convict Chicago crime lord Al Capone of income tax evasion in 1931. It wasn't Elliot Ness and the Untouchables who finally got Scarface—it was the elderly Civil War veteran, Oliver Wendell Holmes Jr.

At Age 87...

Bob Hope
entertained the troops
for the final time.

Born in England, Leslie Townes Hope (May 29, 1903–July 29, 2003) emigrated to America with his family in 1907 and settled in Cleveland. After a brief, undistinguished career as a boxer, Hope started working in Vaudeville, then moved on to star in Broadway, radio, movies, and television. But he will be remembered most for his tireless efforts to entertain American troops around the world. The ski-nosed comedian began his work for the USO performing at California military camps in 1941, before America's entry into World War II. During the course of the war, Hope and his troupe brought laughter to young Americans far from home—on tiny Pacific isles, in vast European encampments, and everywhere in between. Soldiers on remote islands would wake up one morning and find Bob Hope there to entertain them, sometimes accompanied only by a pianist, comedian Jerry Colonna, and the inevitable pretty Hollywood starlet. Throughout the Korean conflict, the Cold War, and Vietnam, Hope's annual holiday tours brought smiles to the faces of new generations of GIs. His final journey took him to Saudi Arabia for Christmas 1990 to entertain the troops of Operation Desert Storm. Hope was honored with the Presidential Medal of Freedom and died in 2003 at the age of one hundred.

At Age 88...

For the first time since 1900, Connie Mack didn't manage the Philadelphia A's.

Born Cornelius Alexander McGillicuddy, Connie Mack (Dec. 22, 1862–Feb. 8, 1956) was a Major League catcher in the 1880s and 1890s, hitting a modest .244. He began his managerial career at Pittsburgh in 1894 and took over the helm of the Philadelphia Athletics in 1901. He was to remain at that post for the next fifty seasons. He owed his job security to the fact that he was a part-owner of the team, but he was also a highly successful manager, at least in the first half of his career. He created two great dynasties (1910–14 and 1929–31) and led the A's to five World Series titles. Financial troubles forced Mack to sell off most of his stars when the Depression began. After 1933, Mack's A's only finished above .500 twice, in 1948 and 1949. In his later years, he wore a business suit and straw boater hat in the dugout, calmly dispensing diamond wisdom to players a quarter of his age. Known as the Tall Tactician, Mack finally retired after the 1950 season with a record of 3,776 wins and 4,025 losses; both totals are records that are unlikely ever to be broken.

At Age 89...

Frank Lloyd Wright began construction on his last great building.

B orn in the Midwest shortly after the Civil War, Frank Lloyd Wright (June 8, 1867–Apr. 9, 1959) became one of the most prominent and influential architects of the twentieth century. After dropping out of the University of Wisconsin, Wright went to Chicago in 1887 to begin his architectural career. He soon won fame for his "Prairie Houses" around the outskirts of Chicago. He designed the great Imperial Hotel in Tokyo, which was completed in 1922, a year before a huge earthquake leveled most of the other large buildings in the Japanese capital—but not the Imperial. His most famous design may be Fallingwater, a unique house in Bear Run, Pennsylvania, that features a stream flowing through it. Wright ignored engineers' warnings that the house wasn't stable; the engineers proved to be correct, and the house later had to be propped up. His last great work was the Solomon R. Guggenheim Museum in New York. He began the design work in 1943, but construction did not begin until 1956, when Wright was eighty-nine. He died in 1959 at the age of ninety-one, a few months before the opening of the Guggenheim.

At Age 90...

Pablo Picasso was honored by the Louvre.

In his later years, Pablo Picasso (Oct. 25, 1881–Apr. 8, 1973) remained as productive and creative as he had been in his prime. He was also prolific in his personal life, fathering four children by three women, only two of whom were married to him when they gave birth. In the late sixties, Picasso turned out a huge number of new paintings and copperplate engravings. Of course, by then anything by Picasso was worth a lot of money, of which Picasso was well aware. He retained ownership of many of his works and died a multimillionaire. His later works were initially panned by critics, who saw them as the demented scribblings of a bitter old man. Only years later were these works recognized as the worthy precursors of a new school of neo-expressionism. In 1971, to honor Picasso on his ninetieth birthday, the Louvre Museum presented a special exhibition of Picasso's work; it was the first time the Louvre had ever exhibited the work of a living artist. Picasso died in 1973 at the age of ninety-one, but his work lives on—and at a high price. In 2004, his painting *Garcon a la Pipe* was sold at a Sotheby's auction for a record $104 million.

About the Author

When he was Mark Washburn's age, the Earl of Cardigan led the Light Brigade to disaster at Balaclava. Mr. Washburn has never been responsible for any military catastrophes that he is aware of, but he has authored a number of fiction and non-fiction books whose publishers may have regarded them as disasters.

A native of Ohio, Mr. Washburn studied history at Princeton, where he received the F. Scott Fitzgerald Award for Creative Writing, and at Duke University. A sometime teacher and editor, he is best known for his non-fiction science writing, including books about the Viking mission to Mars and the Voyager mission to the outer solar system. He is also the author of several novels. He currently resides in Philadelphia.

Happy Birthday!